TOMORROW'S WORLD

HOW TO BUILD A HUMAN

HOW TO BUILD A HUMAN

Written by
Scott Goldie

Illustrated by
Brian Anderson

First published in 2026 by Hungry Tomato Ltd, F15, Old Bakery Studios, Blewetts Wharf, Malpas Road, Truro, Cornwall, TR1 1QH, UK.

Editor: Millie Burdett
Graphic Designer: Sam Fleetwood
Cover Designers: Amy Harvey and Sam Fleetwood
Consultant: Liu Zheng

With thanks to Nicola Carthy

A CIP catalog record for this book is available from the British Library.

Information in this book is up to date as of the time of writing.

ISBN: 9781835694633 (soft cover)
ISBN: 9781835694817 (hard cover)

Printed and bound in China

Discover more at
www.hungrytomato.com

CONTENTS

Chapter 1:

WELCOME TO THE HUMAN BODY!

HOW TO START A BOOK ON THE HUMAN BODY?

What about with... ***what exactly is a human?***

Now, you *probably* are human, but maybe you've never thought about what *being* human means. It's also possible you're something else entirely, like an alien, or a dolphin, or a really clever dog, and you would just like to know about this fascinating species. That's okay too. So, let's ask the experts:

WHO'S RIGHT?

They are all right, more or less. Possibly less so when it comes to being a "flake of rust" but then we do have iron (a type of metal) in our bodies, and iron does rust.

Yep, you my friend are **part metal.** *Cool, right?*

LET'S START WITH THE BAD NEWS.

Our world is full of hazards. Not as dangerous as anywhere else in the universe (after all, Earth has air, and water, and it's a cozy temperature in most places), but it's still pretty dangerous. There are...

- **Bacteria** trying to get inside your body (some are welcome, some are not)
- **Viruses** trying to get inside your cells! (more on cells later)
- **Fungi** that want to live on or in you (and we're not talking mushrooms)
- **Animals** with sharp teeth and claws (e.g. lions)
- **Venomous animals** (e.g. snakes and spiders)
- **Parasites** (animals that want to live inside you – ick!)
- **Accidents** (e.g. falling off your bike)
- **Diseases and illnesses** caused by other stuff (e.g. pollution, aging, and our genes – more on those later too)

THE GOOD NEWS?

Well, firstly your body is brilliant at fighting off all sorts of **nasties,** the term that scientists *definitely* use for harmful bacteria, viruses and fungi (most scientists may in fact call them **pathogens**, but I'm sure that some - the really clever ones - call them nasties). Your body can also heal damaged parts and you even have an organ that can regrow most of itself.

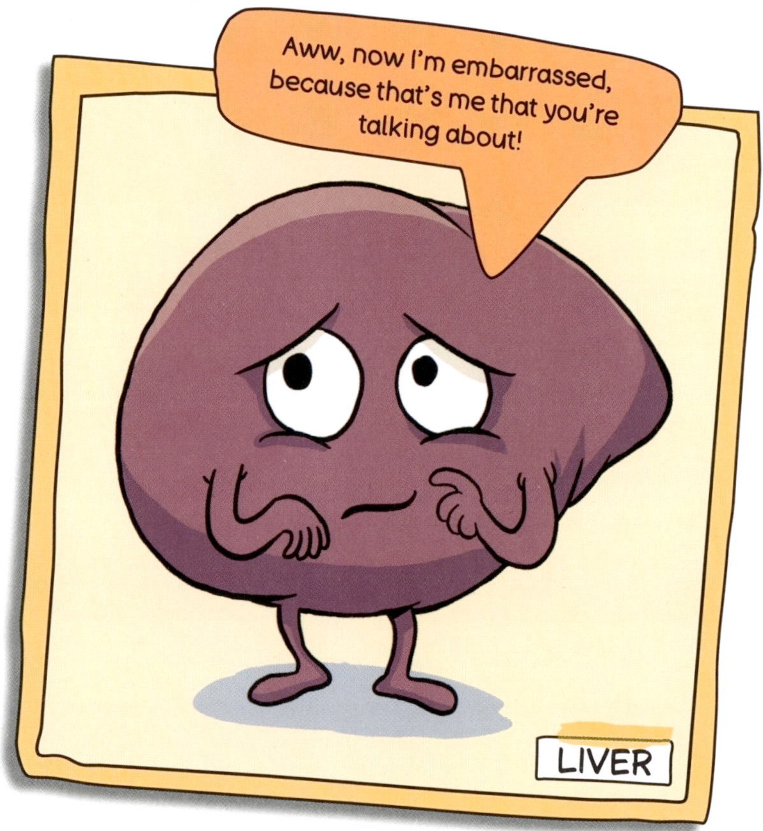

Secondly, doctors and scientists are understanding more and more about our bodies and how they work. This information is being used to develop new techniques to save lives.

Let's take a look at some now!

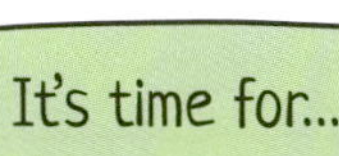

It's time for...

FOUR FACTS AND A FIB!

Can you spot the made-up fib lurking among the true facts?

1) "Superpowered" human cells have been added to a patient's body. These live longer, sneak around almost invisibly, and are better at taking out nasties.

2) Tiny cell-sized robots (nanorobots, or nanobots; nano means really tiny) have been sent into a human body to repair injuries.

3) AI (artificial intelligence) is being used to help develop new medicines.

4) Doctors are using special 3D printers to create and replace damaged bony bits in your body.

5) Brain implants are helping blind patients to "see" again.

Answer: Number 2 isn't true... quite yet. Other types of nanotechnology (or tiny-tech as I think of it) are already in use – but nanobots are still a few years away.

WE MUST BE PATIENT!

Science is truly amazing. However, it's important to remember that it could be many years before some of the advances mentioned in this book are in everyday use.

SO, WHERE ARE WE GOING WITH THIS?

In this book, we'll spend a lot of time inside the human body. Think of it like a guidebook to a new country, with you as a tourist.

YOU MAY BE ASKING YOURSELF...

Why would anyone want to know what happens inside the human body? Humans are disgusting, right? They make horrible smells and have horrible habits. Like picking their noses, looking at what they've picked, and then flicking it at other humans... **GROSS.**

And that's just the outside. Why would we want to look inside at the really icky bits? Well, there are lots of very good reasons for taking a peep.

OUR BODIES ARE FASCINATING

By studying the body, we can answer all sorts of questions...

1) How do we know when it's cold?

2) Why do we have one brain, one heart, one liver... but two kidneys?

3) Which organs can we live without?

4) Why do we dream?

5) What exactly is the point of hiccups?

FUN FACT:

Charles Osborne started hiccupping in 1922 and didn't stop until 1990, 68 years, or about 430 million hiccups, later. That's the longest case ever. The worst thing about it? We don't even know why we hiccup!

OUR BODIES HELP US ANSWER BIG QUESTIONS

Some of these questions include:

1) Where did humans come from?

2) How similar are we to other animals?

3) How do the organs in our bodies talk* to each other?

4) How do cells know what to do?

5) Should I have a cheese and tomato or a peanut butter and jelly sandwich?

*Organs do not talk. Communicate may be a better word.
All good questions, except number 5, because eating peanut butter and jelly is just weird.

OUR BODIES HELP US LEARN ABOUT ILLNESS

By finding out about our bodies, we can discover what to do when things go wrong. Broken bones, infections, diseases, a bite from a poisonous snake… we can find the solutions to these problems by exploring inside our bodies, asking questions, trying out ideas and finding amazing answers.

This is probably a good place to point out that trained doctors explore bodies, usually dead ones (dead bodies, not dead doctors). I'm not suggesting that you should try and answer questions this way, especially ones like, "What colour is my liver?"

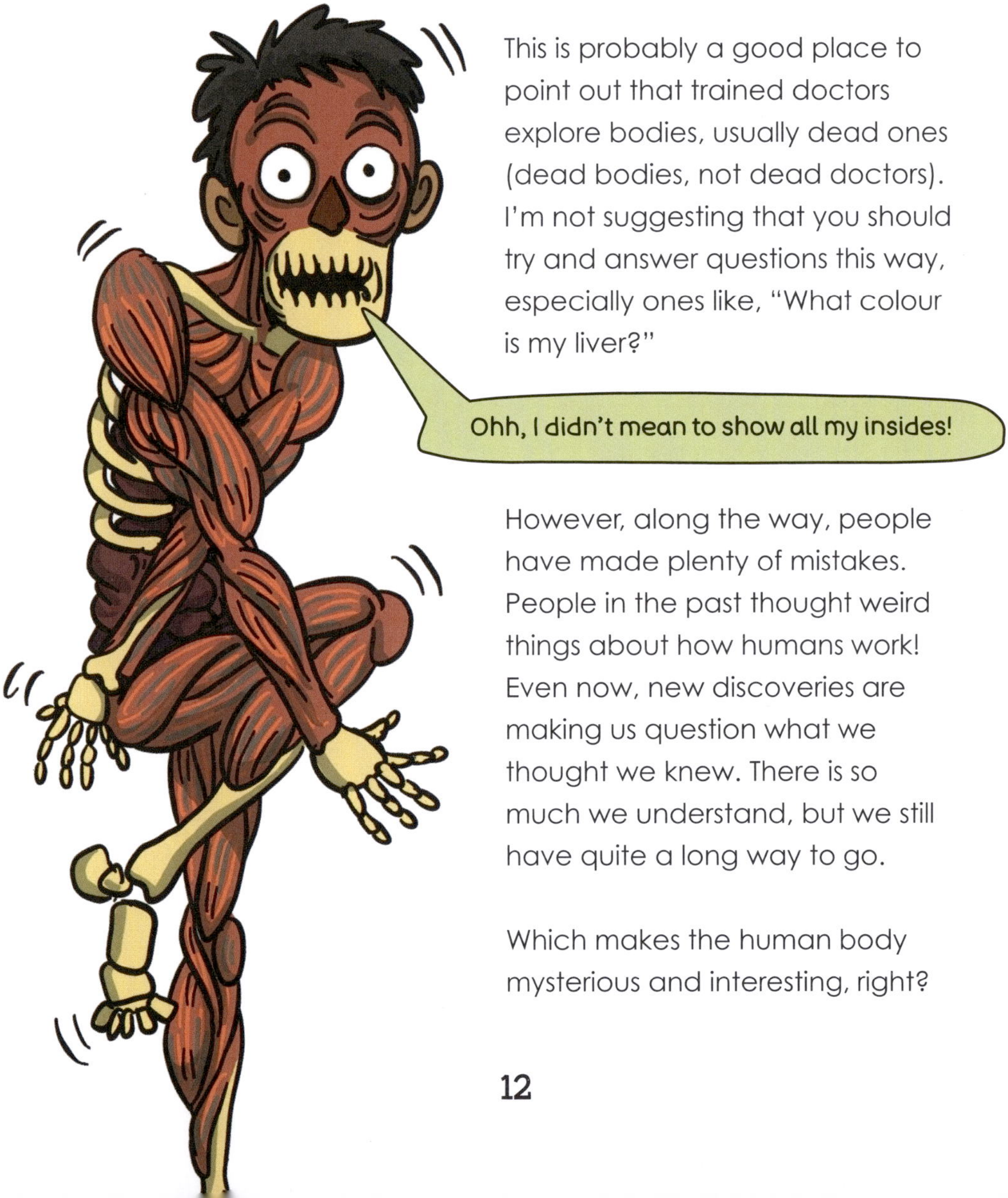

However, along the way, people have made plenty of mistakes. People in the past thought weird things about how humans work! Even now, new discoveries are making us question what we thought we knew. There is so much we understand, but we still have quite a long way to go.

Which makes the human body mysterious and interesting, right?

So, where do humans come from? And how could we make our own? Let's wipe off the dust and get out the recipe book...

HOW TO MAKE A SMALL HUMAN:

For an adult human, double the ingredients.

YOU WILL NEED:

- 18 kg (40 lbs) of oxygen
- 6 kg (13 lbs) carbon
- 3 kg (6.6 lbs) hydrogen
- 1 kg (2.2 lbs) nitrogen
- 600 g (1.3 lbs) calcium
- 300 g (0.66 lbs) phosphorus
- Approx. 60 g (0.13 lb) each of: potassium, sulfur, sodium, chlorine, and magnesium
- A pinch of: boron, chromium, cobalt, copper, fluorine, iodine, iron, manganese, molybdenum, selenium, silicon, tin, vanadium, and zinc

HOW TO MAKE:

STEP 1

Find an empty planet with water – not too hot or cold.

STEP 2

Empty the ingredients into the water.

STEP 3

Sit back and wait for about 3,700,000,000 years (that's 3.7 billion, or thereabouts).

STEP 4

Cross your fingers! You may end up with a human... or more likely something else, like a fish-lizard or a bird-insect or a sea cucumber (that's an actual real animal). Or you could end up with zilch. Even after all that waiting, nothing may have happened.

You see, we understand what ingredients are needed to create a human (the 25 essential elements, as they are known), but those ingredients are not alive. *We* are alive. The big mystery is how those lifeless ingredients created life. So, we need an initial spark of life* followed by a few billion years of adaptation. That's how you could make a human.

*There are several ideas about where the initial spark of life came from, including deep-sea volcanic vents and comets!

FUN FACT: OVERFLOWING ELEMENTS

There are more elements in the human body than the essential 25, maybe as many as 59, but many do nothing. Some of them, such as cadmium, are poisonous. Even the essential ones can cause problems: selenium keeps you healthy, but too much can poison your liver!

WHAT IF I CAN'T WAIT THAT LONG?

Okay, because you haven't got 3.7 billion years to wait, what else can you do? Well, if you had all the right *living* parts (brain, heart, bones, and the rest), maybe you *could* build a human...

Let's go through it, step-by-step.

Don't try this at home. The human body is incredibly complex and it's very easy to wire things up wrong... it might also make a fair bit of mess on your bedroom rug!

ASSEMBLING A HUMAN:

1. Start with the frame – that's your bones, muscles, ligaments, etc. Attach these together. Leave the ribs for now, as well as the skull, otherwise it'll be hard to add some of the internal organs.

2. Add the brain to the skull. Fit the skull onto the rest of the skeleton, making sure it attaches to the spinal cord (which runs through your backbone).

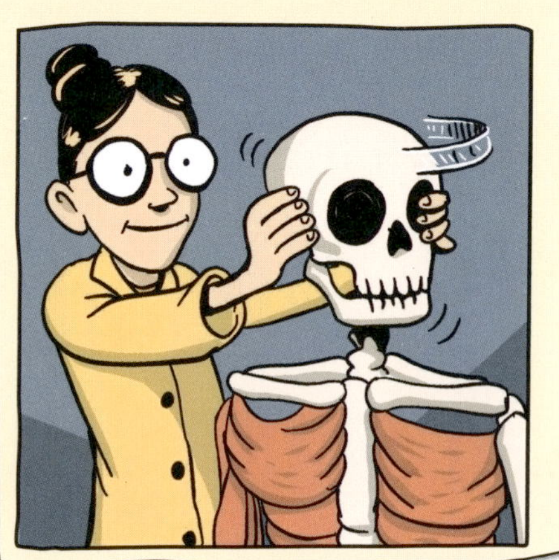

3. Attach the senses (e.g. the eyes in the eye sockets, the tongue in the mouth) and connect these to the brain with nerves.

4. Put in the heart. Add all of the tubes that come with it (the arteries, veins, and capillaries). There's a lot of these but don't rush it – every part of the body must have its own supply of blood.

5. Add the other organs: the lungs, liver, kidneys, spleen, etc. Make sure you connect them up so that organs that need to 'talk' with each other can do that easily.

6. Add the other bits and pieces needed – the soft tissues, the fat, the glands to make hormones, that sort of thing. It's really important that nothing is left out.

7. Add the skin. Connect up all the nerves (careful, there are a lot of these!)

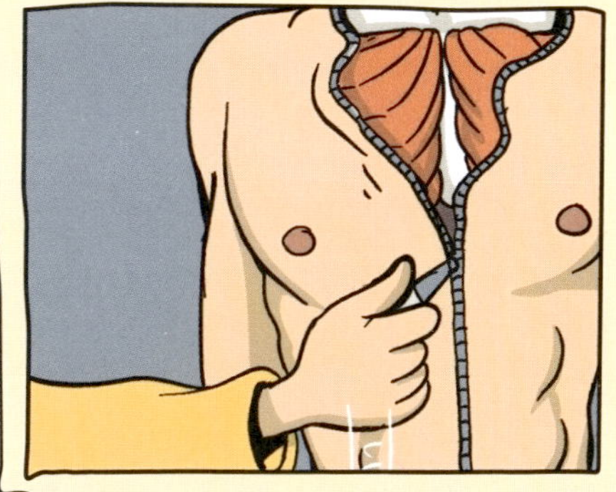

8. And... that's it! One human! Say hello to your new friend!

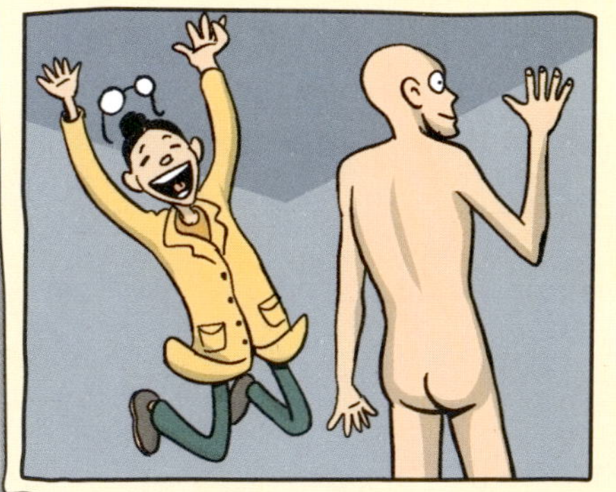

SO WHAT ARE WE MADE OF?

Your body is made from organs (heart, brain, etc) and tissues (muscles, bones, etc) – but what are they made of? The answer is… **cells!**

What is a cell? Well, let's play…

FOUR FACTS AND A FIB!

Can you spot the hidden falsehood lurking among the true facts?

1) There are about 30,000,000,000,000 (30 trillion) cells in your body. If you're an adult, it's roughly 37 trillion.

2) You have more than 200 different cell types, each with their own jobs.

3) Every one of cells in your body is alive.

4) Each cell contains a "code" that only you have.

5) You have another 30 trillion cells (or thereabouts) in your body that are not really yours at all…

Worked out the answer yet?

Answer: Number three is the fib. Cells are living things but every second (yep, every second), millions of your cells die and are broken down by other cells, so your body contains many, many dead cells. Which means… wait… number five is true?

Let's take a look at the facts:

HOW MANY CELLS?!

Yep, your body really is made from about 30 trillion cells (please don't try to count them).

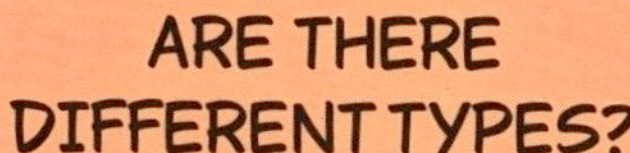

ARE THERE DIFFERENT TYPES?

There are at least 200 different types of tiny cell in your body. Some live for a long time, while others only survive for a few days. Some move around the body, others stay put. When a cell dies, all of the other cells gather round and says nice things about the cell. This is followed by a moment of silence, followed by a cell-ebration of their life!

IS EVERY CELL IN YOUR BODY ALIVE?

Not really. When a cells die, certain other cells pounce on them, gobble them up, and break them down into bits for recycling. That's happening right now, all over your body. And that's okay. It's meant to happen. The cell has done its job and, when its time has come... it's time for other cells to do theirs.

WHAT DO OUR CELLS CONTAIN?

Inside most of your cells is a special code – let's call it DNA (because that's its name). This tells your cells what to make and teaches your body how to grow. Many cells keep this code inside a tiny blob called the nucleus, and in other places too.

Cells use parts of this code to do important stuff. It's a bit like a tiny recipe book, with thousands of recipes that do all sorts of clever things.

LET'S TALK MORE ABOUT DNA

All life on Earth uses DNA. About half of the recipes that your body uses are also used by carrots. And approximately 90% of your recipes are identical to those used by cats. Weird, right?

But it's the differences in our DNA that matters. These differences are what give you much less body hair than a cat and a much larger brain than a carrot.

SO HOW DO SCIENTISTS STUDY DNA?

Is the code interesting to look at, like a secret spy code written in invisible ink that only reveals itself on a full moon and takes many years to crack?

ANSWER:

Er... yes? (not quite honest answer). And no (honest answer).

You see, the code is made from only four letters: G and C (which always pair up) and A and T (which also hang out together). Many parts of your own code will look like this:

GCATGCGCGCATATGC...

SO HOW DO SCIENTISTS KNOW SO MUCH?

Well, there are two reasons. And then another two.

1. They are clever,
2. They are hard-working,
3. They don't mind staring at the same 4 letters for hours,
4. They've spent years researching.

LET'S TAKE A LOOK AT SOME OF THE BIG PROJECTS:

NAME?
The Human Genome Project

WHEN?
1990 – 2003

FOUND OUT ABOUT?
The parts of DNA that different cells use to make their special recipes.

NAME?
ENCODE

WHEN?
2003 – well, it's still happening... DNA is pretty complex, you know!

FOUND OUT ABOUT?
The bits of DNA that do not have cell recipes (which is most of DNA, to be fair).

NAME?
The Human Cell Atlas

WHEN?
2016 – when those scientists say they've finished!

FOUND OUT ABOUT?
How cells "talk" with each other. The clever scientists also discovered new types of human cell – amazing, right?

NAME?
The International Human Microbiome Standards

WHEN?
2012 – this is a keeper; it's not going to stop!

WHAT DO THEY WANT TO DO?
Make sure all scientists from across the world use the same rules and measures when they talk about the microbiome (that's the other stuff that lives in you!)

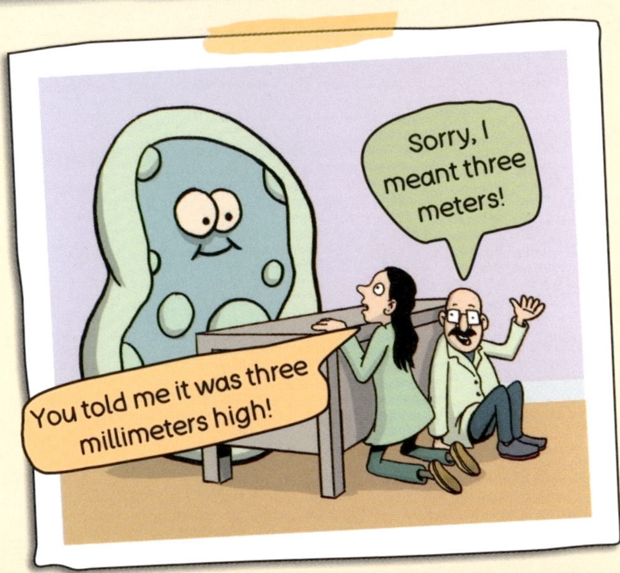

SO NOW IT'S TIME TO LOOK AT THOSE OTHER LIFE-FORMS INSIDE YOU.

I'm sure you're full of questions, like...

WHAT ARE YOU TALKING ABOUT?

DO I REALLY WANT TO KNOW ABOUT THEM?

WHY HASN'T MY BODY DONE SOMETHING?

Easy, easy! Don't panic. Yep, there's a lot of other stuff inside you, but that's okay. It's actually really helpful, and your body would not function well without it.

That's not to say there aren't some nasties inside you right now, because there probably are. But your cells are doing a brilliant job of hunting them down and destroying them, which has the added benefit of keeping your tiny personal army well-trained and ready for action.

So, what is supposed to be there? Well, your body contains about 30 trillion non-human cells in your mouth, your intestines, on your skin, up your nose (pretty much everywhere, in fact). Does that make you half-human, half-whatever? Not really, because these single-celled creatures are even tinier than one of your cells!

In fact, all 30 trillion of them add up to about the same mass as your brain, or about one-third of a cat.

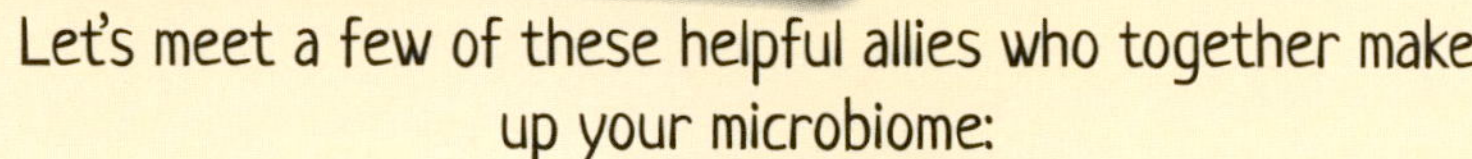

Let's meet a few of these helpful allies who together make up your microbiome:

BACTERIA

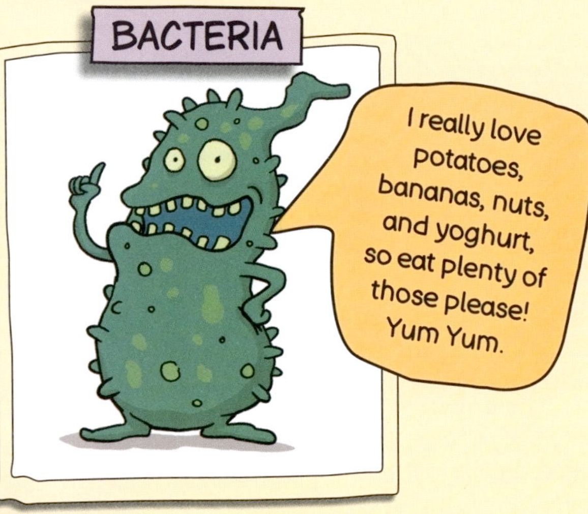

Bacteria lives in your large intestine, where it's warm, cosy, and has everything it needs. It helps to break down food and also makes useful vitamins for us.

FUNGUS

Please don't sneeze me out!

This little fungus lives in your nose, helping keep things nice and clean, and breaking down dead cells.

PROTOZOA

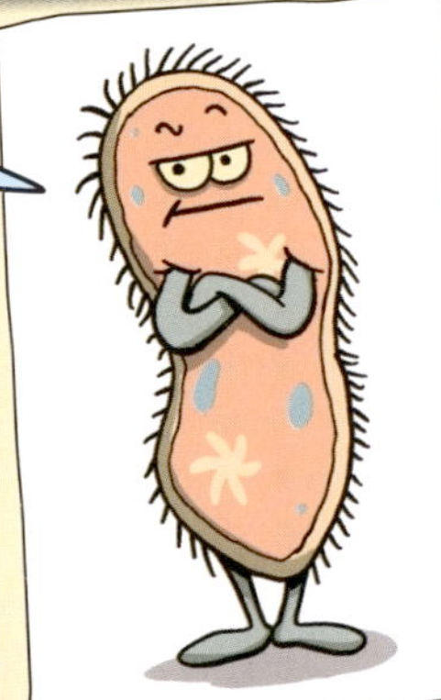

Protozoa also lives in your large intestine, and gobbles up any bacteria that could potentially make you sick.

Let's end this section with something simple: **homeostasis.**

TOP TIP:

Homeostasis what? I can hear you trying to say this and it's coming out as gibberish - so just, stop! **Try breaking it down like this:**

HO - ME - OH - STA - SIS

Without you having to lift a finger, your body controls...

TEMPERATURE:

Your body keeps you cozy. You sweat when you're hot and shiver when you're cold.

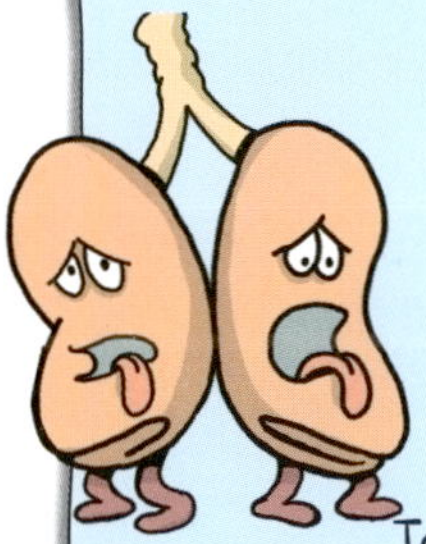

BREATHING:

You breathe faster when you exercise because you need more oxygen.

EATING AND DIGESTION:

Telling you when you're hungry, or full, or need a poo. (Or all three at once).

DRINKING:

Telling you when you are thirsty, or need to pee.

SLEEP:

It tells you when to go to sleep, and when to wake up.

There's also other stuff that happens without you thinking: your heart beats, your lungs contract and expand, your eyes blink, your food is digested... Your body balances itself so you can concentrate on doing more enjoyable things.

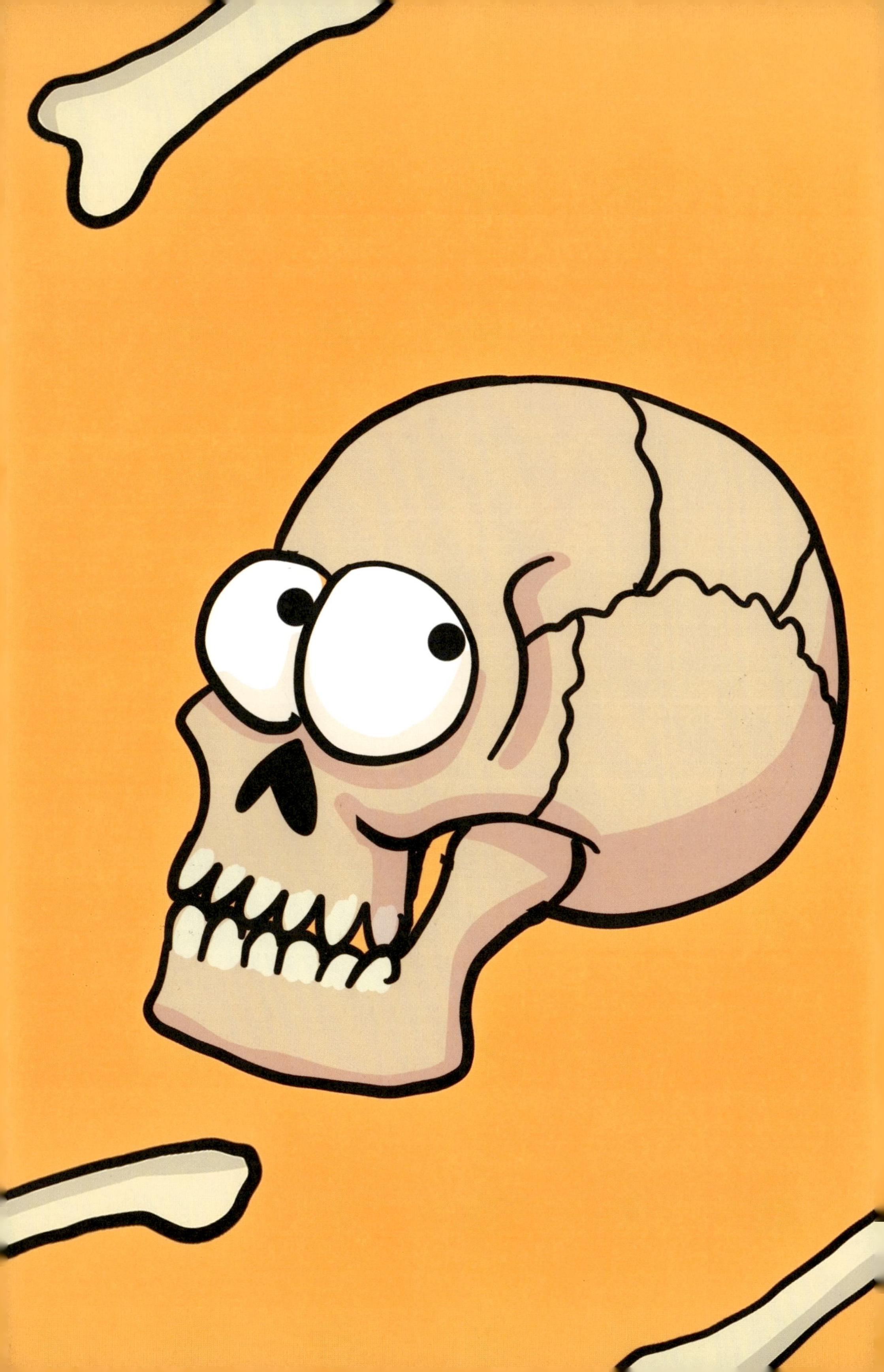

Chapter 2:

BUILDING A SKELETON

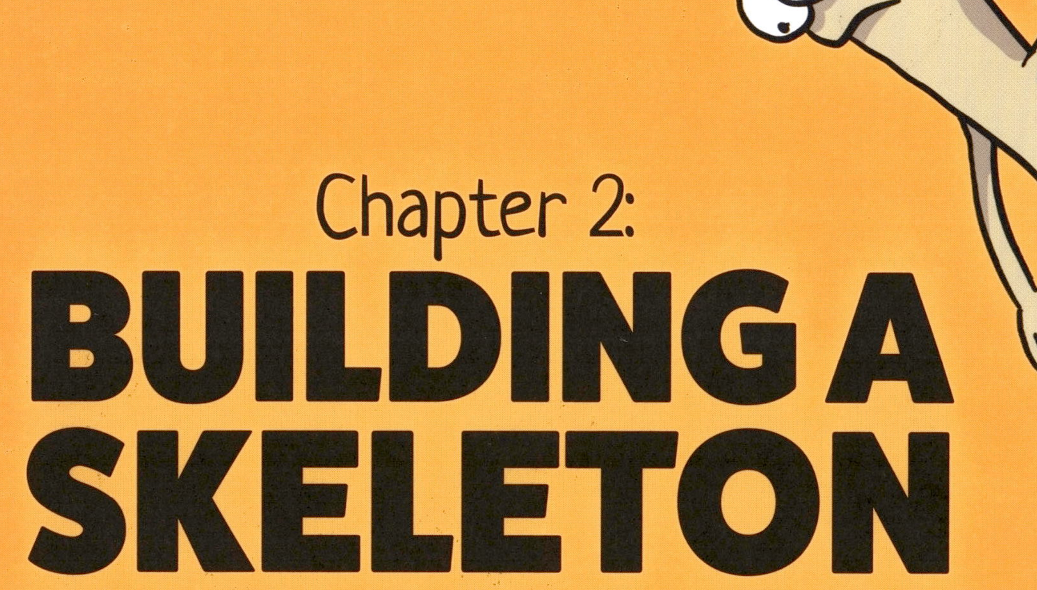

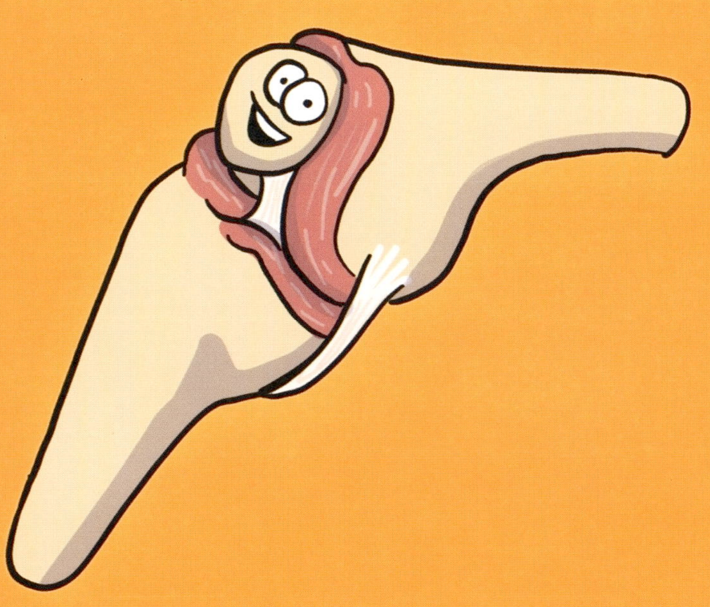

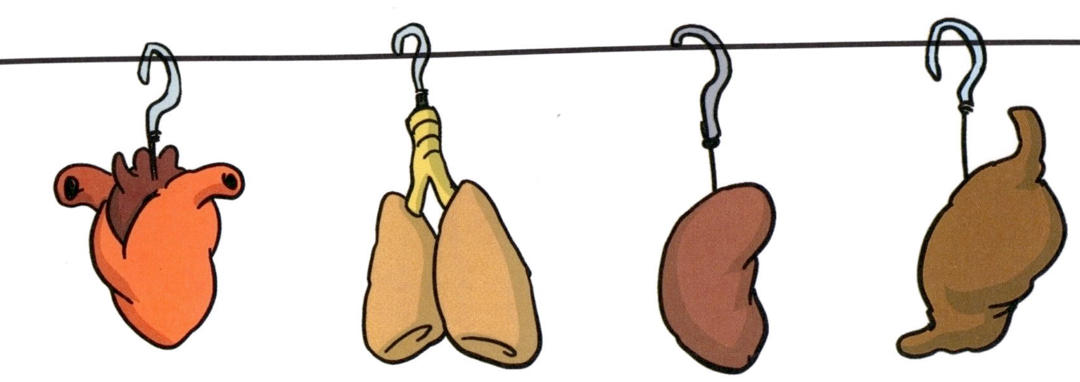

LET'S START FROM THE BEGINNING:

If you were to build a human, it would be sensible to start with the skeleton. It gives you a frame to hang the other bits off.

Also, the skeleton has staying power. The other bits rot away, but the skeleton hangs around for years, centuries even. Maybe it's only fair that we reward this commitment by starting here!

SO WHAT ACTUALLY ARE WE?

Humans are mammals and mammals are **vertebrates** (so are fish, birds, amphibians, and reptiles). Only vertebrates have internal *inside* skeletons, or backbones.

OUR SKELETONS ARE VERY IMPORTANT. THEY...

1) stop us from being shapeless blobs,

2) protect the squishy bits (e.g. the heart, lungs, and the brain),

3) work with our muscles and allow us to move,

4) are not always solid – all sorts of exciting stuff happens inside them!

5) store calcium, which is needed for healthy bones. And when other body bits are running low, they can steal calcium from the bones.

BONES ARE BRILLIANT, BUT THEY DON'T COME WITHOUT THEIR PROBLEMS:

1) Bones are not very flexible and can break.

2) Joints can wear out.

3) There are diseases which affect our skeletons, including arthritis, which causes joint pain and swelling.

NEED SOMETHING FIXED?

Sometimes our bodies need help, so it's just as well that scientists have got our backs! Get it? Because there are bones in your back! Hilarious I know.

JOINT REPLACEMENTS:

When a joint (e.g. the hip or knee) is affected by arthritis or gets worn out, the damaged bone is removed and parts made from metal, plastic, or ceramic are added instead!

3D PRINTING:

Doctors can print out pieces of bone-like material or use "inks" that include living cells to fill gaps or breaks in bones. Over time, these "biomaterials" slow dissolve and are replaced with actual bone.

PROSTHETICS:

These replace missing parts of the body, such as a leg or hand. More complicated prosthetics actually link to the brain or skeleton. At Chalmers University of Technology in Sweden, scientists have created bionic hands that connect to nerves and muscle. Patients can actually feel what they are doing using their artificial hands! Prosthetics can be made from all sorts of stuff. David Aguilar from the USA was still a teenager when he made himself the first working prosthetic limb... using LEGO!

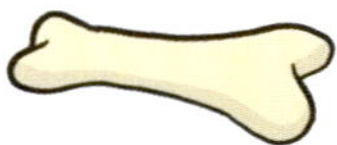

BABY BONES:

The Wellcome Sanger Institute in England has been finding out about the skeleton before we are even born. This could help scientists find treatments for problems, such as when bones in the skulls of babies join together too early, or identifying genes connected to arthritis.

NANOTECHNOLOGY:

Tiny particles target damaged bones (such as a broken arm) and reinforce the break, making it stronger. Just like with 3D printed bones, they'll stay just long enough for the bones to repair themselves, and then they'll disappear.

In the future, nanobots (tiny robots) could travel into the human body, find bone breaks, deliver medicine, and help speed up repairs. Who wouldn't want mini-robots whizzing about inside their body?

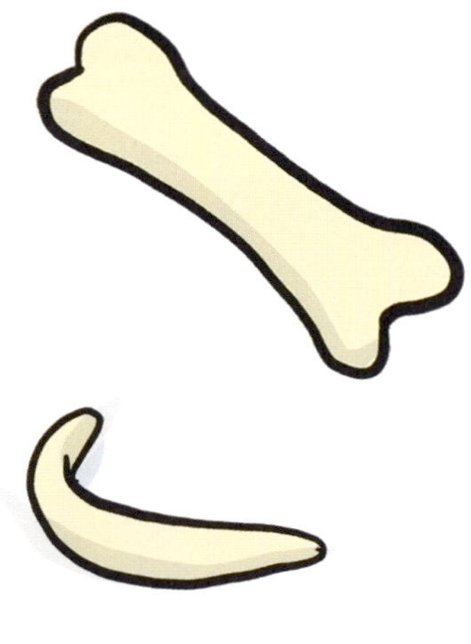

LET'S BREAK IT DOWN:

There are 206 bones in an adult skeleton, although a newborn baby actually has about 270 bones. As we grow, some bones are lost.

Not "lost", as in "Silly, careless babies! Who ever trusted them with 270 bones in the first place?" Lost as in they join together, several smaller bones growing into one larger bone.

But why, I hear you say, is it not just one part in the first place? Well, there are two reasons. One, your brain was still growing and the separate bones meant it didn't get squashed. Two (and slightly ickier), the bones allowed your head to change shape when you were born. Human babies have large heads (because humans have large brains) and this flexibility makes it safer for both baby and mom.

BEFORE YOU WERE BORN

Way, way before you are born, your whole skeleton was actually made from cartilage. Cartilage is not as strong as bone, but is more flexible and grows more quickly. Your nose, ears, and voice box are still made from cartilage.

TRY THIS:

Gently tug at your ear. Is it bendy? Can it be shaped in different ways? If it can't... are you sure it's your ear? You also have cartilage at the ends of your bones. In fact, cartilage is so brilliant that sharks have an entire skeleton made from it – and they've been around since before the dinosaurs!

AFTER YOU WERE BORN

By the time you were born, most of your skeleton was made from bone. However, your kneecaps only fully change from cartilage to bone when you're three years old. In fact, your body will still be replacing cartilage with bone when you're a young adult!

LET'S BONE UP ON SOME MORE SKELETON FACTS!

YOUR SKELETON IS ALIVE:

Your bones are constantly being made and broken down. In fact, it takes only ten years or so for every cell in your skeleton to be replaced. Bone-eating cells called osteoclasts break down parts that we do not need anymore, releasing the calcium, while bone-making cells called osteoblasts take this calcium and use it!

INSIDE THE BONE:

Tiny osteocytes connect together inside the bone. They warn the other bone cells of any problems and generally keep an eye on things. (Well, not really an eye. Cells don't have eyes.)

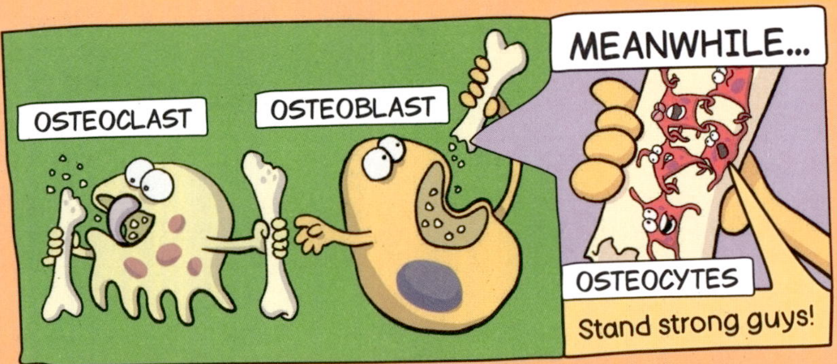

BONE BAR

No gravity? No problem!

KEEP ACTIVE!

In space, astronauts have to exercise for three hours every day. Their bone-making cells take a break due to the lack of gravity but the bone-eating cells carry on as normal, which makes their bones incredibly weak.

SOME BONES ARE BIG:

The femur, or thigh bone, is the largest bone in your body.

SOME BONES ARE SMALL:

The smallest bones in your body are in your inner ear and are vital for hearing. They are called the anvil, the hammer, and the stirrup, which is only 3 mm (0.1 inches) long – the same length as the average ant. They are named after their shapes, not because a tiny blacksmith lives in your head.

SOME COME IN GROUPS:

There are 33 bones in your back called vertebrae which allow you to stand upright in a way that no other ape can. There are also 27 bones in each hand and 26 bones in each foot, meaning that half the bones in our bodies are in your hands or feet.

SOME ARE ON THEIR OWN:

The horseshoe-shaped hyoid bone is beneath your chin. It is the only bone not directly connected to the rest of your skeleton. Muscles and ligaments hold it in place instead.

THERE ARE TWO TYPES OF BONE:

CORTICAL

Cortical, or compact, bone covers the outside of the bones. This is the stuff that makes bones look white and smooth. The only thing harder in your body is the enamel covering your teeth!

CANCELLOUS

Cancellous bone is spongy and full of holes. It's found in larger bones: your hips and your vertebrae (back bones) The spaces are actually created by bone cells which massively swell up before dying, leaving a cavity behind.

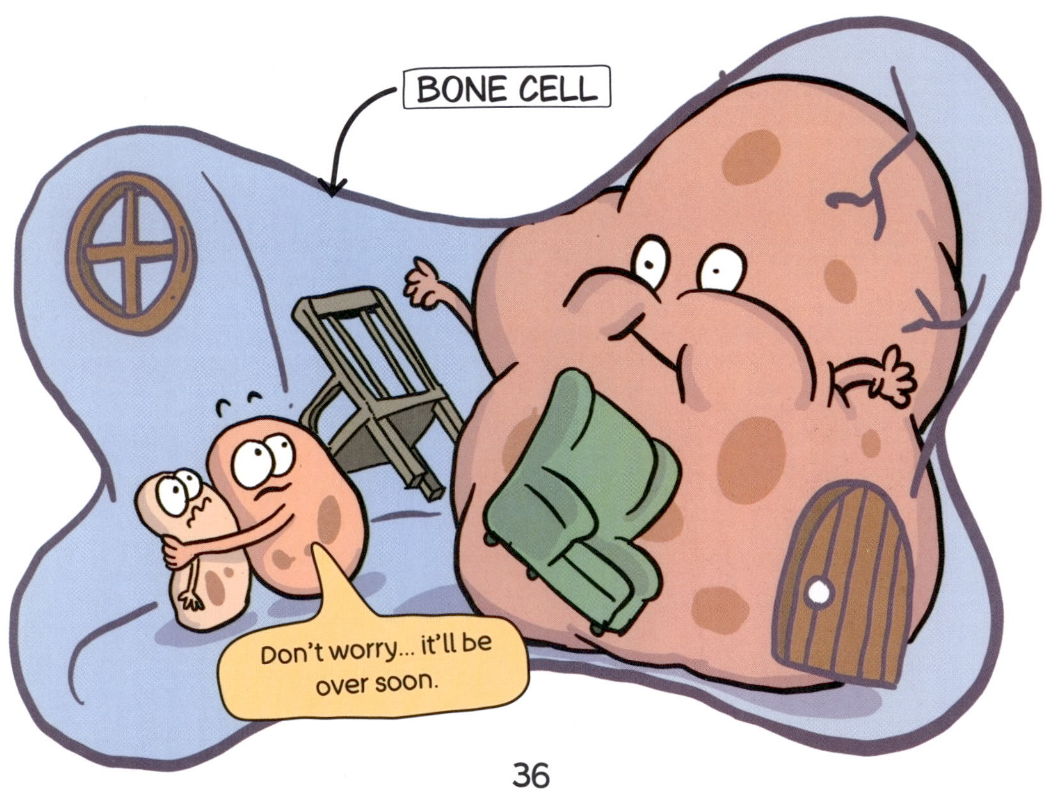

Spongy bone is flexible, meaning that you can run and jump, and the shock of your landing is absorbed. The spongy bone is also filled with two types of bone marrow:

YELLOW MARROW

Found in: long bones, such as the femur (thigh bone)

Contains: fat cells

RED MARROW

Found in: the ribs and shoulder blades

Contains: stem cells

Stem cells are found throughout the body. Most cells can only create an exact copy of themselves, but these clever little things can make more than one type of cell. The stem cells in your bone marrow can make red blood cells, white blood cells, or platelets, depending on what your body needs.

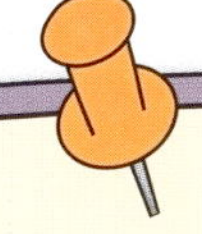

IMAGINE THIS:

You fall off your bike (don't try this out) and hurt your knee. It starts bleeding. Platelets are needed to help make a scab. Your body sends a message* to the red bone marrow.

*this message arrives as a chemical called a protein, not as an email or a text!

Your bone marrow is incredibly busy. It creates billions of red and white blood cells and platelets every day. That's about two million new red blood cells every second.

THERE ARE THREE TYPES OF JOINT:

Bones meet at a joint. They are held together by ligaments – tough fibers which keep the bones in place.

FIBROUS JOINT

You'll find this joint between the different parts of the skull. This type of joint is unable to move. They are knitted together like one of your grandma's cardigans.

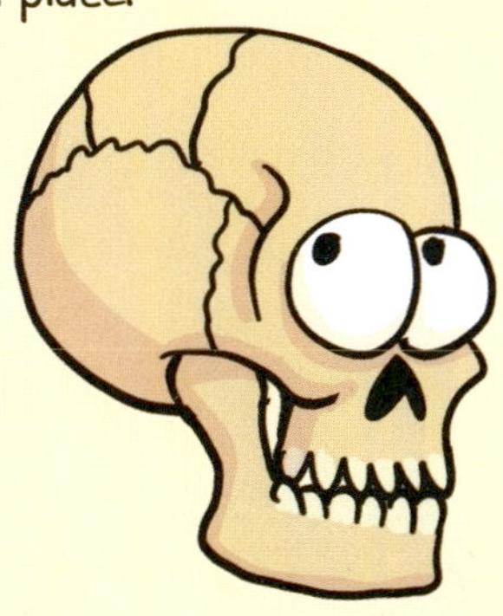

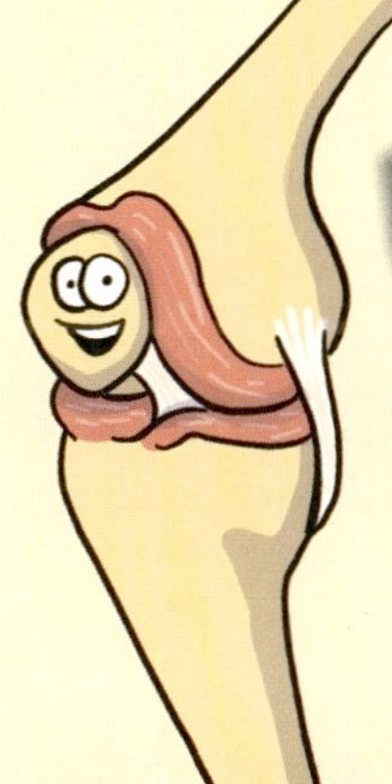

SYNOVIAL JOINT

This joint comes in six different types, including hinge, pivot, and ball and socket. Your knee is your largest synovial joint. Each one of these joints is covered by tough gristle, and makes an oily liquid to stop the bones wearing out. Clever!

CARTILAGINOUS JOINT

This joint uses cartilage to join bones together, like how your ribs connect to your sternum (the bone down the middle of your chest) – this allows your chest to expand when you breathe in.

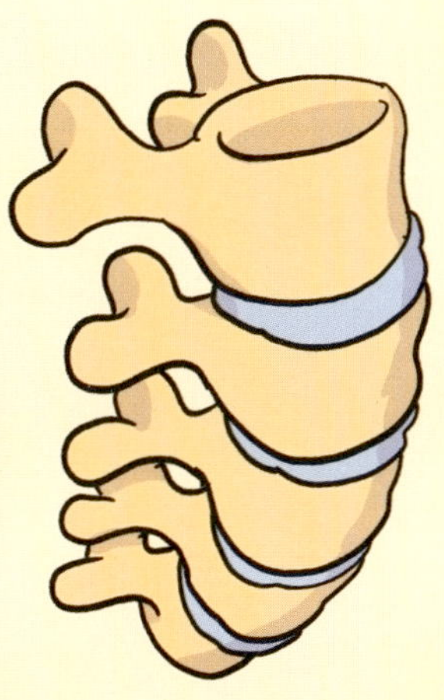

HOW MANY MUSCLES DO WE HAVE?

Your body has over 600 muscles! You could not move without muscles. They allow you to walk, keep your heart beating, and help you digest food. Together, your skeleton and the muscles make up over half of your body weight!

Muscles can do two things: **contract** or **relax.** And they can only pull, not push. Even when you push open a door, your muscles are *pulling* your bones. Muscles normally work in pairs.

IMAGINE THIS:

When you contract your biceps in your upper arm, your lower arm moves up. When you relax your biceps and contract your triceps, your arm moves back.

SO WHICH ONE IS THE BIGGEST?

The largest muscle is the **gluteus maximus** (yep, it's a muscle, not a Roman Emperor) which is found in your bottom, and helps you walk upright and climb stairs. The smallest muscles are in your inner ear, where the smallest bones are.

THERE ARE THREE TYPES OF MUSCLES:

CARDIAC MUSCLES:

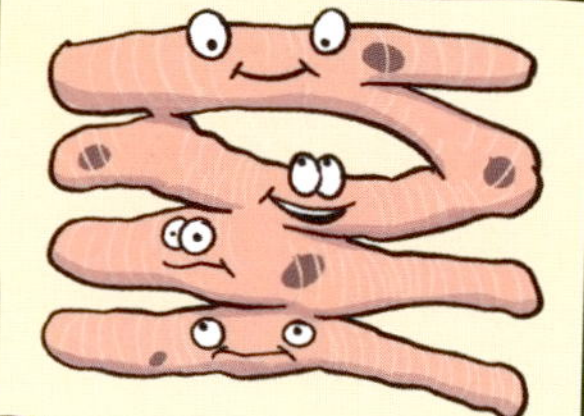

These can be found in your heart and keep the blood pumping.

SMOOTH MUSCLES:

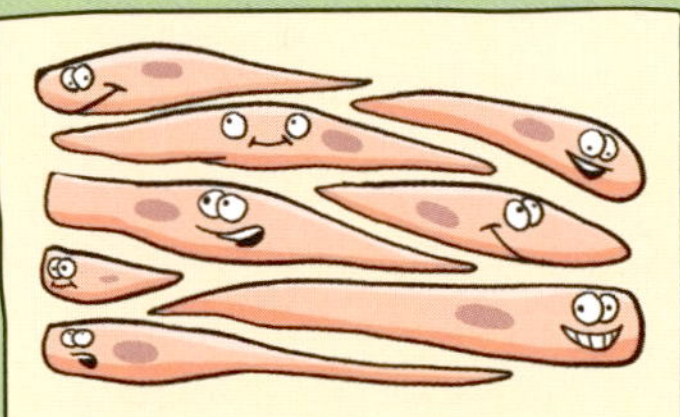

These are found inside your gut and blood vessels. You don't even have to think for these muscles to work!

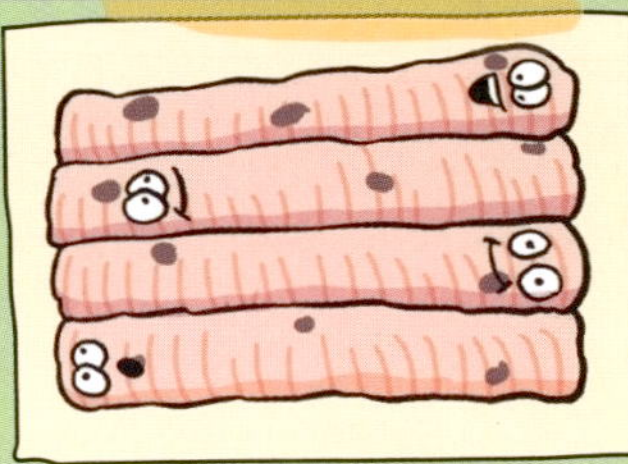

SKELETAL MUSCLES:

These muscles attach to the bones and allow you to walk, swim, and play computer games!

Muscles are attached to your bones by tough cords called **tendons**. One end of the tendon attaches to the bone and the other end to the muscle. The strongest tendon is the **Achilles tendon**, which connects your heel to your calf (the muscle in your lower leg, not a baby cow). There are no muscles in your fingers, only tendons. A tiny tendon in your inner ear even attaches the smallest muscle in your body to the smallest bone. Sweet!

Then there's the fascia, which is a network of connective tissue that covers the muscles and holds them together.

KEEP MOVING!

To keep your skeleton and muscles healthy, you need to exercise. Your bones continue to grow until you are about 25 years old. But things don't stop there. The process of replacing your bones lasts for your whole life and exercise helps to keep these bones strong.

Cycling, dancing, playing sports, hill walking, gardening, yoga: pretty much anything that makes you tired will be good for your muscles and for your bones.

Be careful, though! Exercise too vigorously, move or twist suddenly, or forget to warm up first, and you could injure yourself. Muscles can be strained, ligaments and tendons torn, and bones can be broken. And all these things take time to heal! It is also really important to eat a balanced diet, full of the things that your bones and muscles need.

YOUR BONES AND MUSCLES NEED...

CALCIUM: a mineral essential for strong bones. Found in dairy products, leafy greens, figs, and fortified foods such as bread.

VITAMIN D: helps our bodies absorb calcium. We get vitamin D from sunlight and from oily fish, eggs, and dark chocolate.

 **PHOSPHORUS:** helps calcium build strong bones. Found in meat, dairy products, seeds, and nuts.

 **PROTEIN:** about half of our bone structure is made from protein. Protein is also vital for healthy muscles. Found in meat, dairy products, nuts, beans, and pulses such as chickpeas.

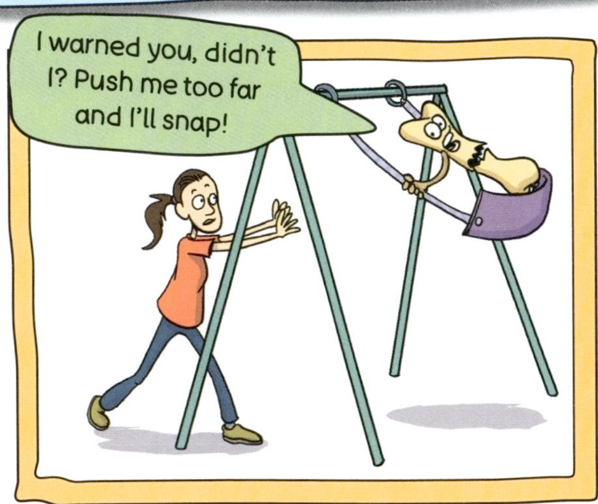

Our skeletons are designed to put up with a lot. But push them too far and something's got to give. Sometimes, that something is a bone!

Children are light and their bones are flexible. Just as well, because they are always falling off or over things! About half of children break a bone, usually the clavicle (collarbone) or the bones in the arm.

THE GOOD NEWS?

Bones heal fairly quickly.

THE REALLY GOOD NEWS?

Children's bones heal very quickly because children are still growing. Bad breaks may need an operation, but usually a sling, a splint, a cast, or even a special kind of boot are enough. (Only if you break a foot bone. If you break your arm and your doctor offers you a boot, find another doctor!)

LET'S LOOK AT WHAT MIGHT HAPPEN IF YOU BROKE SOMETHING:

(We're talking bones here, not a pencil or your favorite cup.)

1 You tumble off your bike and land badly on your arm. Something snaps. Ouch!

2 At hospital, an X-ray is taken. A type of radiation passes through your arm giving a picture of what's happening inside. The bones in your lower arm – the radius and the ulna – are both fractured. You'll only need to wear a cast for a few weeks.

3 You are given painkillers. A kind doctor makes sure your bones are in the right position.

4 Layers of material are wrapped around your arm, gradually hardening into a plaster cast which keeps your bones straight.

5 Now for the clever bit. You've never broken anything before, but your body knows exactly what to do. Bone-eating cells are busily destroying the damaged bone. Other cells make a callus of soft cartilage over the break. Gradually, this is replaced by a hard bone-like callus, after which the cells use bone to repair the break.

6 About 6-8 weeks after you fell, the cast comes off. Your arm is fixed! Be careful though: it'll be months, or even years, before the bone is completely healed.

LET'S END THE CHAPTER WITH TEETH!

Teeth are part of the skeletal system, but are not made from bone. Humans have two sets of teeth, the first being milk teeth, but many animals have far more.

Most children have 20 milk teeth by the age of three. From about the age of six, these begin to fall out and are replaced by adult teeth. This can take years, and some adults do not get their wisdom teeth until they are thirty, or even older. Some do not grow wisdom teeth at all. A full set of adult teeth includes 32 teeth.

It is important to brush teeth regularly, usually twice a day for about two minutes. This adds up to nearly one whole day of brushing every year!

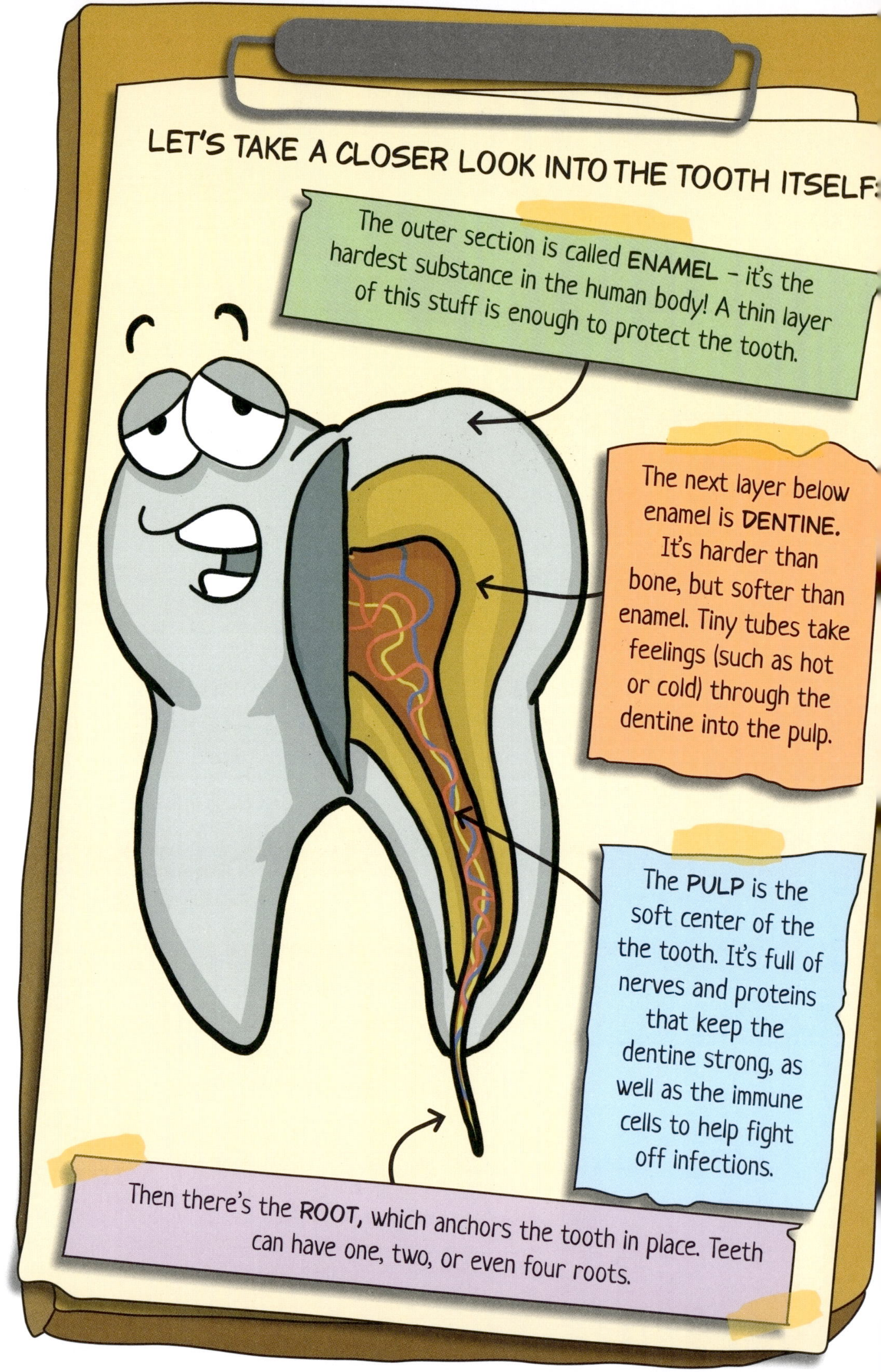
LET'S TAKE A CLOSER LOOK INTO THE TOOTH ITSELF:
The outer section is called **ENAMEL** – it's the hardest substance in the human body! A thin layer of this stuff is enough to protect the tooth.
The next layer below enamel is **DENTINE.** It's harder than bone, but softer than enamel. Tiny tubes take feelings (such as hot or cold) through the dentine into the pulp.
The **PULP** is the soft center of the the tooth. It's full of nerves and proteins that keep the dentine strong, as well as the immune cells to help fight off infections.
Then there's the **ROOT,** which anchors the tooth in place. Teeth can have one, two, or even four roots.

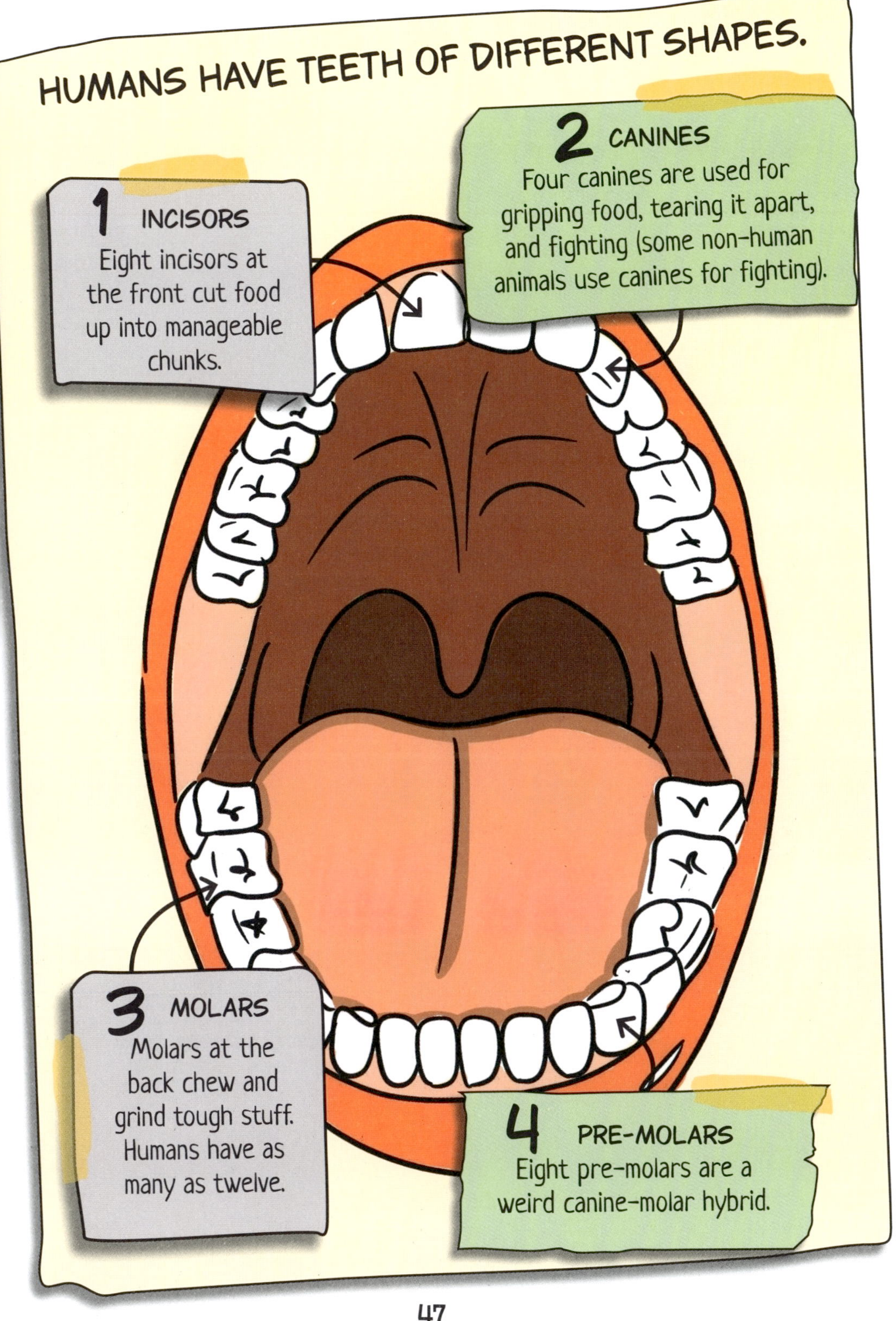
HUMANS HAVE TEETH OF DIFFERENT SHAPES.
1 INCISORS
Eight incisors at the front cut food up into manageable chunks.
2 CANINES
Four canines are used for gripping food, tearing it apart, and fighting (some non-human animals use canines for fighting).
3 MOLARS
Molars at the back chew and grind tough stuff. Humans have as many as twelve.
4 PRE-MOLARS
Eight pre-molars are a weird canine-molar hybrid.

Chapter 3:

DON'T BE NERVOUS... TIME TO ADD THE BRAIN!

Now that the skeleton's all done, it's time to add...

THE NERVOUS SYSTEM.

And no, your nervous system isn't the bit in your body that makes you worried. Well, it is that bit, but it's so much more. Your nervous system is the control center. It does all your thinking and feeling, even when you are not aware that you are thinking or feeling.

IT'S MADE UP OF THREE PARTS:

1 Sensory organs collect information about the outside world... and the inside world (i.e. your body).

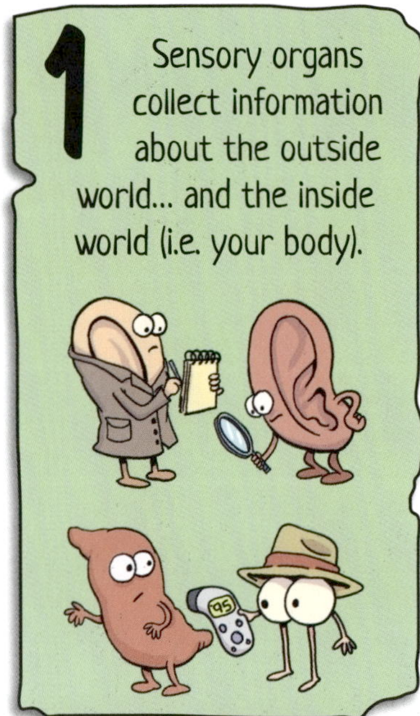

2 Nerves take signals from the organs to the brain, and back again.

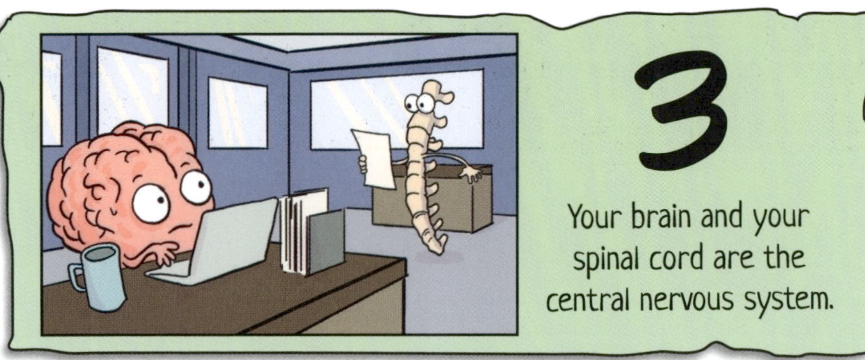

3 Your brain and your spinal cord are the central nervous system.

A human brain is made of 60% fat. Your brain is a lump of wrinkly tissue which looks a lot like a walnut.

Your brain makes sense of the world even though it's trapped inside your skull and will never get to see that world. It tells you when you're hurt, although it doesn't feel any pain itself.

Your brain has around 86 billion cells, which is about the same number as the stars in the Milky Way. These cells, or neurons, are connected in a great web made up of trillions of tiny links. When you think, or dream, or talk, chemical and electrical signals race around your brain. Walnuts don't do this.

And your brain is constantly changing, making new connections, these pathways growing stronger as you practise new skills.

IT'S AN INFORMATION HIGHWAY!

Your spinal cord is about 42 centimeters (17 inches) long. It's protected by the vertebrae in your back and takes information from your body to your brain. It contains about one billion neurons and can control simple movements and reflexes without having to check with the brain first.

Every day, your brain sends more messages than all of the phones in the world. It generates enough electricity to power a lightbulb (don't think about trying that out – you need this electricity!)

The human brain is very complex and scientists are still learning how things connect together. But the amazing thing about your brain is its ability to adapt and learn, and that's being used to create something awesome.

BRAIN COMPUTER INTERFACE

I am talking about a device called brain-computer Interface (BCI for short). You can probably work out what it means for yourself – connecting up a brain and a computer (or maybe a robot arm), and using the power of your thoughts to make things happen (such as the robot arm moving). Brilliant, right?

This technology has been developed over many years. At first, back when computers were much bigger, the devices were not user friendly. Now, the technology is much smaller. And it has the power to change lives.

BCIs are being used for people who've lost the ability to move their arms, letting them pick things up and manipulate them. People who are paralysed (unable to move) could use implants to communicate what they want, such as, "please close the window" or "play some music."

Electrical signals are sent from the device to train the brain, which learns what they mean. The brain can then send messages back and the computer makes sense of them!

There are two different types of BCI – implants and wearables. **Let's take a look at them:**

HOW DOES BCI WORK?

Implants are fitted onto the brain. Tiny threads – thinner than a human hair – are inserted into parts of the brain.

IMPLANTS

POSTITIVE	NEGATIVE
The brain-device connection is strong.	• It needs an operation. • The body can "reject" the device

Wearables sit somewhere on the head, maybe like a pair of glasses. They send signals through the skull into the brain.

WEARABLES

POSTITIVE	NEGATIVE
• No operation needed! • The device can be put on...and taken off!	The brain-device connection is not as strong because of interference from the skull.

An adult brain weighs around 1.3 kg (2.9 lb) - about the same as twelve large hamsters. Although it makes up a tiny fraction of your body's total mass, it uses at least 20% of all the energy you get from your food.

Think about that. If you ate five biscuits (please don't - it's two biscuits too many), one of those biscuits would just be for keeping your brain powered. In fact, children's brains are even more demanding, using up to 40% of all the energy your body needs (or two biscuits out of every five).

Yep, your brain is a very hungry organ.

PARTS OF THE BRAIN

The brain is split into several parts, and each part has a different job. Let's take a look at the main brainy bits:

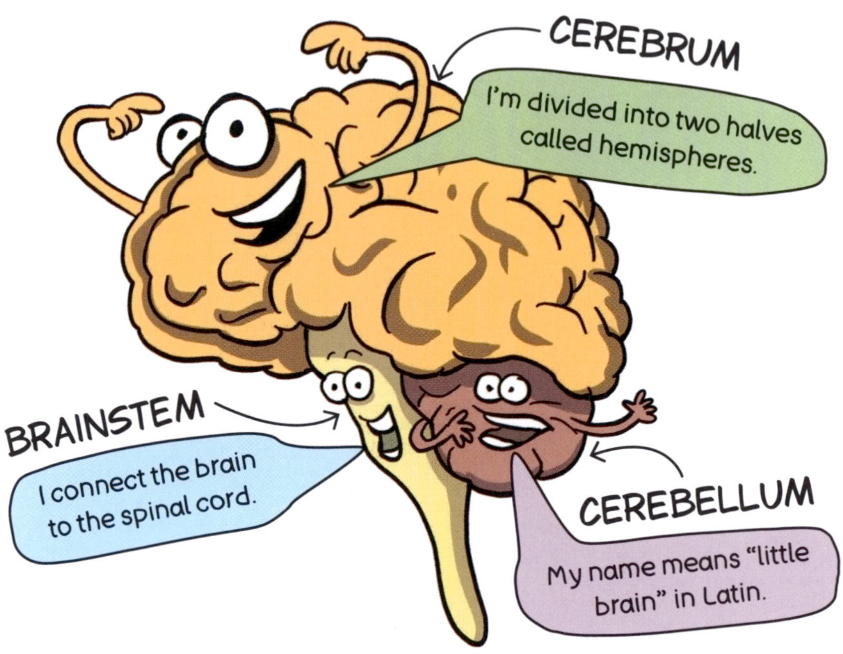

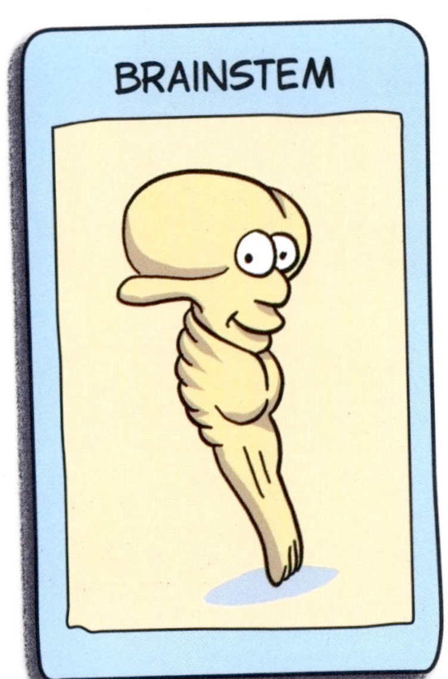

BRIEF DESCRIPTION: I'm only little! Find me near the back of the brain.

JOB: I do stuff so you don't need to think about it: breathing, keeping your heart beating, sweating to keep you cool, sleeping, and waking up. Every piece of info from your body to your brain and from your brain to your body goes through me! I'm like a really busy train station.

TELL US A JOKE: How did the cerebrum say hello? It sent a brain wave!

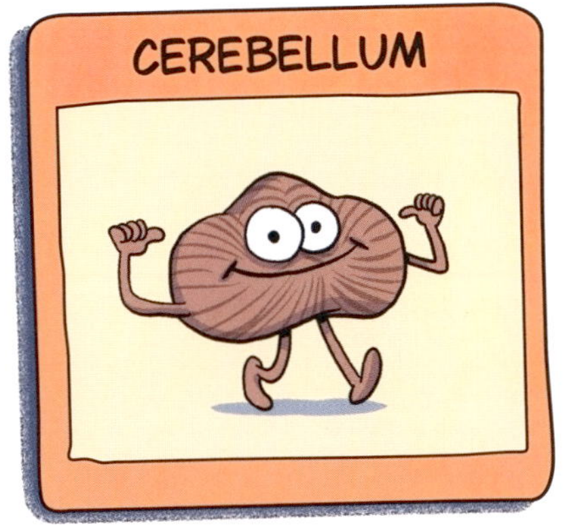

BRIEF DESCRIPTION: I'm tucked away, folded under your cerebrum. If you unrolled me (which I'm not saying is a good idea), I'd be about 100 cm (39 in) long and 5 cm (2 in) wide.

JOB: I help you catch balls and stay upright when you run, but I do other things too, like working out what hurts, making sure you're not overcome by fear, and helping you pay attention.

TELL US SOMETHING INTERESTING? Sorry, what were you saying? I lost focus there.

BRIEF DESCRIPTION: I contain 15 billion cells. My left hemisphere is logical and likes to solve problems. Its favourite subject is math. My right side prefers art and music: it's creative and emotional. The right hemisphere controls the left side of the body and the left hemisphere… I'll leave you to work that out.

JOB: Jobs, you mean? I do your thinking, planning, working out what you're going to say - important stuff like that. Without me, you could not read this book. Or even know it was called a book. I make sense of the world – what you see and hear - in different regions called lobes. My outer layers are gray (they're called "gray matter", often used as a name for the whole brain), but I'm actually white inside.

DREAM DESTINATION? I'd like to see Italy. Well, not see it, but I'd like to make sense of the visual input I get using my occipital lobe.

FEELINGS AND THE BRAIN

AMYGDALA

This part of the brain is almond-shaped (amygdala means almond in Greek) and is part of the cerebrum. It makes sense of feelings, especially fear, anger, and enjoyment. It also links emotions to events to help you remember things more clearly.

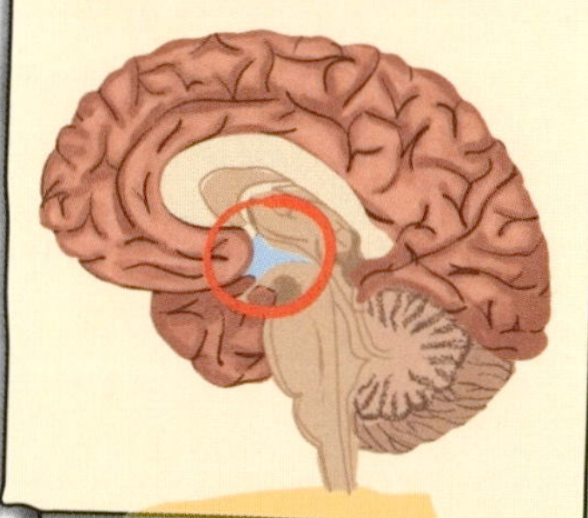

HYPOTHALAMUS

This part of the brain is only the size of a blueberry, but it's really important! It controls how hungry you are, how hot or cold you feel, and whether or not you need sleep. It works closely with the pituitary gland to control all sorts of other body bits!

HIPPOCAMPUS

There's two of these, one on each side of your brain. And no – they're not hippo-shaped! They're about the size of your thumb and help you make memories, find your way around, and make sense of the world.

Fun Fact: John O'Keefe, May-Britt Moser, and Edvard I. Moser received a Nobel Prize in 2013 for discovering how cells in our hippocampus help us to navigate; a bit like a map in our brains!

WHAT IS THIS BRAINY STUFF MADE FROM?

Well, a brain cell is called a neuron. Most of your neurons are in your brain but there are billions more throughout your body, adding up to a massive 100 billion, or possibly more.

Humans have about 86 billion neurons in their brains. That's a lot! Other animals have nowhere near as many. One species of tiny worm has only 102 neurons and even animals that are larger than humans, such as lions and giraffes, have fewer neurons than us.

In fact, one human brain has roughly the same number of neurons as...

- one thousand hamster brains (90 million neurons each)
- one hundred cat brains (760 million neurons each)
- three chimpanzee brains (28 billion each)
- one-third of an elephant brain (257 billion each)

That's right! Elephants have more brain neurons than you! So why aren't elephants cleverer? Well, because you have many more neurons in your cerebrum, the thinking part of your brain.

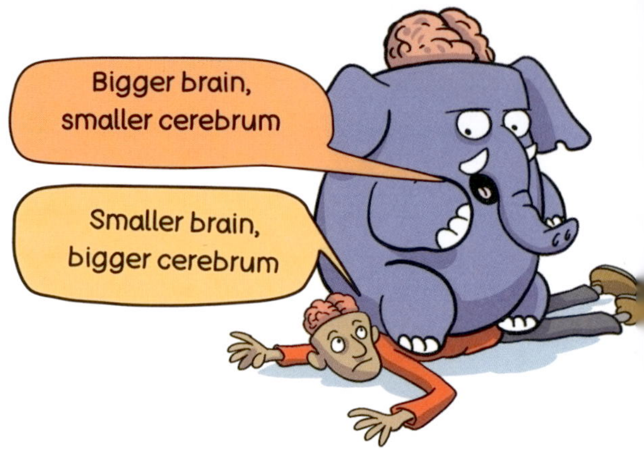

YOUR BRAIN IS ELECTRIC!

NEURON NETWORK

Neurons create a network that connects every part of your body. Each neuron reaches out with long finger-like tendrils that almost actually touch each other. They have tiny gaps between called synapses. Signals or messages are sent through these synapses using chemicals and tiny bursts of electricity which travel at about 120 meters (390 ft) every second! That's why when you stub your toe, you feel the pain very quickly.

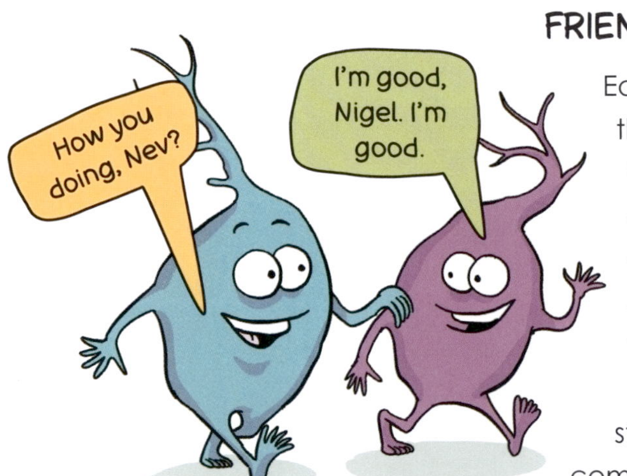

FRIENDLY CONNECTIONS

Each neuron can have thousands of connections. It's like being friends with everybody in your school all at once, and being able to send messages to any of them. Just like people, neurons build stronger connections if they communicate more regularly.

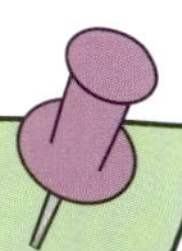

It's time for...

FOUR FACTS AND A FIB!

Can you spot the made-up fib lurking among the true facts?

1) Your brain knows where all the messages in your body are coming from. It knows how often the signal is being sent and decides what action is needed, if any.

2) The longest nerve in your body is about 1 meter (3.3 ft) long, traveling from your foot all the way to the bottom of your spinal cord!

3) Unlike other cells, neurons do not divide.

4) Adults lose about 100,000 of their neurons every day.

5) Your neurons do not live long. Within a few months, they're exhausted, and die.

Answer: Number 5 is not true. Neurons are with you for a long time — in fact, some you'll keep your whole life! Parts of them are replaced when they're worn out, but each neuron keeps on doing its job for many years!

NO PICTURES PLEASE!

Neurons are like film stars! They grab all of the attention and they're all we ever hear about when the brain is mentioned. But the thing is, the neurons don't do it all on their own. Just like famous actors need hairdressers, make-up artists, and people to work the cameras, neurons need other cells to do the jobs that they are too busy to do.

That's where glial cells come in. These cells are also part of the nervous system but they do not send signals around your body. Instead, they play really important roles in keeping everything running smoothly. They look after the neurons, making sure that they can focus on the job that they have: sending signals. Once neurons have found their place to be, they stay put. They do not move. Some glial cells travel around, whilst others find a particular neuron to hang out with.

FUN FACT:

There are actually more glial cells in your nervous system than neurons.

LET'S MEET A FEW OF THESE FRIENDLY GLIAL CELLS!

ASTROCYTE:

These cells look like tiny stars! They have several very important jobs, including repairing injured neurons and feeding them when they are hungry. These jobs certainly keep them on their toes! Not that they have toes...

MICROGLIA:

These cells are tiny little shapeshifters! They gobble up anything that shouldn't be there, such as nasty bacteria. They also snip away at any weak, unused connections between neurons. If neurons are damaged beyond repair, they get gobbled up too!

SCHWANN:

Schwann cell can be found in most parts of your nervous system, but not your brain or spinal cord. They wrap themselves around the nerves and produce a substance that does not conduct electricity. This allows the signals between neurons to stay clear and strong.

BUSY BUSY BUSY!

Your brain is bombarded with information every second. Your eyes tell it things they can see, your ears tell it what they can hear, your nose... you get the idea!

So why isn't your brain – and why aren't you – overloaded by everything?

Well, that's because your clever brain filters through this information and decides what you can ignore. It also tells you what it thinks is important, and leaves you to decide what to do about it.

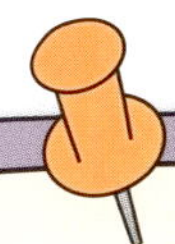
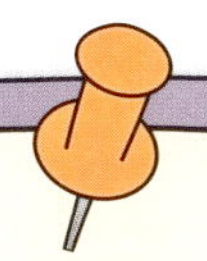

IMAGINE THIS:

Sometimes, something can snatch at your attention. For example, you might be talking to your friends at school and someone else from another little huddle of people nearby says your name. And you hear your name; it rings out clearly like a bell! That's because your brain has been sort of secretly listening to the other conversation but decided you could ignore it, until your name was mentioned!

And this is very important. Our brains allow us to focus on information important to us. In the past, it may have even saved our ancestors' lives!

Ugg. Ugg!

Huh?

MEMORY COMES IN THREE TYPES:

Not only does your brain filter all of that information, but it also stores important stuff as memories.

SENSORY MEMORY:

What you've just seen, or heard, or felt. Most sensory memories do not last – otherwise your poor brain would quickly get overloaded!

SHORT-TERM MEMORY:

This is information that you hold for about half a minute. You can only store a few things in short-term memory. Try to remember this list: dog, frog, cat, fish, bird, mouse. Practise saying it a few times to help.

LONG-TERM MEMORY:

This is where important short-term memories can end up. In long-term memory, you store facts and knowledge and can recall these when somebody asks you a question, such as, "What are the three big parts of the brain called?" If it's in your long-term memory, you can answer the question. If it's not... well, you can make it up, and hope for the best!

THE BRAIN IS JUST TRYING TO HELP:

We might not like it, but pain is very important. When you hurt yourself, you're finding out what you should and should not do. Pain is your body's way of telling you to stop doing something.

Pain also tells your body to do something. For example, if you cut your finger, the nerves send pain signals to your brain telling it to send platelets and white-blood cells to the cut to stop the bleeding and fight infection.

HOW DO WE STOP THE PAIN?

Painkillers work by blocking the signals in your nervous system. Let's take a look at how that might work.

1. You are putting up a tent. Your job: knock in the tent pegs. Your mallet slips and you hit your thumb. Ouch!

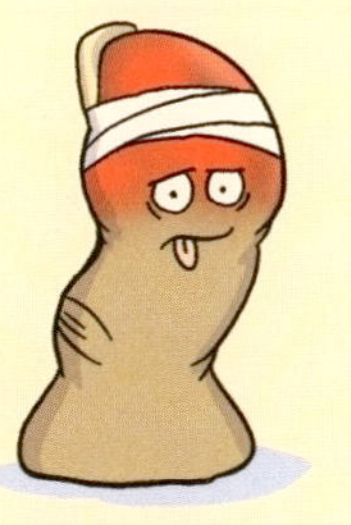

2. Your mom (or dad) decides to give you painkillers. She checks the dose you should have (this is VERY important). You swallow one tablet and wash it down with water.

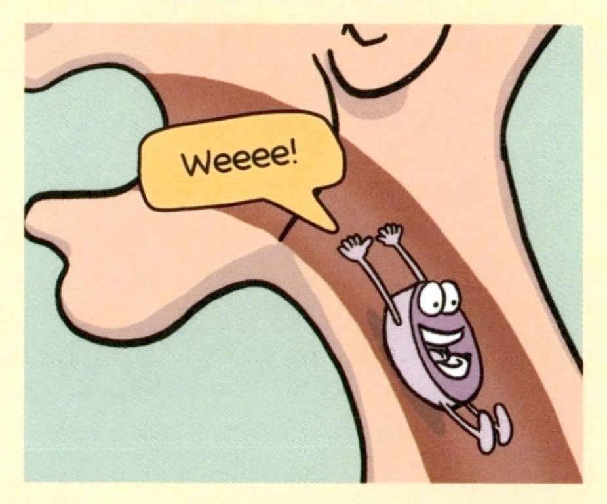

3. The medicine dissolves inside your stomach. A lot of it passes into your bloodstream and travels around your body.

4. The painkiller reaches your thumb. It blocks out some of the chemical signals, reducing the pain and the swelling. It also reaches your brain and works there too. In fact, it goes everywhere in your body. The medicine knows where to work, and where not to!

5. After a while, your thumb does not hurt as much. A few hours later, the medicine has stopped working and your thumb is throbbing again. Your mom gives you another tablet to stop you making a fuss.

That's just enough about the brain. But before we go – without sneaking a peek – can you remember the six animals mentioned earlier? If you can, they may just have snuck into your long-term memory!

Chapter 4:

SETTING UP THE SENSES

Now that your body has a brain, and a skeleton...

LET'S ADD THE SENSES!

Your senses give information to your brain, which then makes sense (ha ha!) of it all and decides what to do. Your brain never gets to see, or hear, or smell the world. It's the organ that makes the big decisions, but stays snug inside your skull!

Most of your senses are on your head. This makes sense because the messages from your eyes or ears do not have to travel all the way up your spinal cord to get to your brain. Imagine if your nose was on one of your feet! Signals from the nose would have to travel through your entire body to give your brain information about interesting or nasty smells.

Your senses are incredibly important. They are also quite complicated, as we'll find out later. There's a lot that can go wrong! But those clever scientists are on the case, exploring all sorts of ideas to restore senses that may have stopped working or are not working as they should.

RESTORING SENSES:

BREAKTHROUGH:
Electronic noses used for smelling.

TELL ME MORE!
Electronic noses, or E-noses, are being developed for all sorts of purposes. Nose-shaped devices use AI (artificial intelligence) to sniff out the bacteria that cause food poisoning, while others sniff out infection or disease. Tiny nasal implants could restore a sense of smell to people who have lost it, or give people a super sense of smell, allowing them to sniff out things that humans usually can't...

BREAKTHROUGH:
Bionic eyes used for restoring eyesight.

TELL ME MORE!
Scientists are developing artificial eyes for patients who have lost their sight. These eyes are actually tiny cameras that send electrical signals to the brain. Currently, they only allow wearers to see light and simple shapes. In the future, these bionic eyes might actually let users see further than human eyes and also allow them see in the dark! Cool!

BREAKTHROUGH:

A very helpful virus used for restoring hearing.

TELL ME MORE!

Scientists are using a harmless virus to help deaf people hear, sometimes for the first time ever! The virus is given some special DNA and then sent deep into the patient's ear to a tiny pea-sized organ called the cochlea which is lined with cells. The virus repairs the hairs on these cells, allowing the patient to hear again! Amazing!

HOW DO WE SEE THINGS?

Our eyes are incredible little spheres evolved over millions of years. Our eyelids blink about 14,000 times a day, which means you spend over 20 minutes blinking every day! Eyelids help keep our eyes moist, remove any bits of dust, and protect our eyes from bright light.

WHY ARE OUR EYES SO IMPORTANT?

We actually get more information through our eyes than all of the other senses put together, so sight is often thought be our most important sense. We have two eyes to give us binocular vision, meaning we can judge distance. This is so we can tell the difference between a toy elephant up close and a real living elephant far away.

SO HOW DOES SEEING WORK?

Well, let's find out, using a small purple grape.*

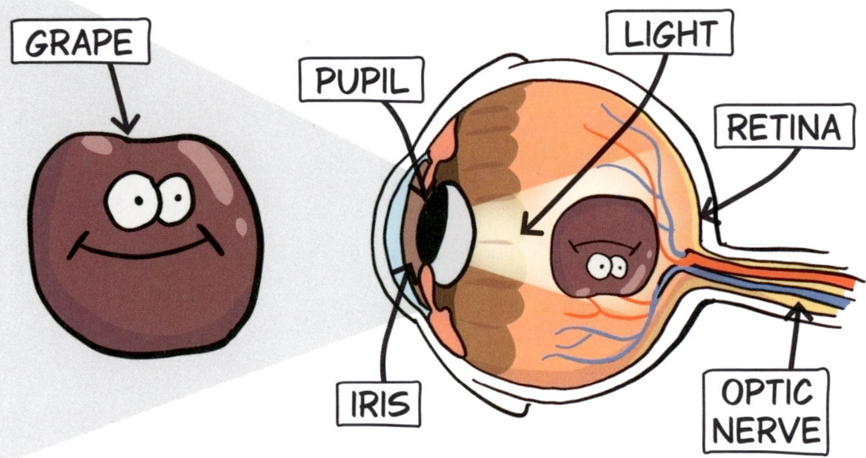

*Yes, I know it's only a picture of a grape. Use your imagination!

1. Light bounces off the grape. This light enters your pupils, the black circles at the center of each iris (the colored bit). Your brain makes your pupils larger or smaller, depending on how dark or light it is.

2. The light hits the retina, the lining at the back of each eye. Here, there are over 100 million cone cells, coming in three colours: red, blue, and green. They get excited when they see their color: red cones by red, blue cones by blue, green by... you get the idea. Purple is a mixture of red and blue.

3. Each retina also contains about seven million rod cells. These detect how much light there is, whether anything is moving, and are particularly important for seeing in darkness or at night.

4. The information from the cone and rod cells travels along your optic nerve, which contains about a million nerve cells. It reaches your brain.

5. Your brain thinks, "Huh. A grape."

We can see about one million different colors. However, not everybody has the same number of cones and some people may not have red or green cones, meaning that they cannot see certain colors. Some people have no blue cones, meaning that the world appears a mixture of reds, greens and whites. People who have missing cones have a condition called color-blindness.

FUN FACT:
Because of the way that light enters our eyes, we actually see the world upside down! (Imagine all those upside down grapes.) It's our clever brain that flips it the right way around for us.

WHY DO SOME PEOPLE NEED GLASSES?

Most people (about two-thirds) don't have perfect (or almost-perfect) eyesight. Eyes don't always grow exactly the correct shape, meaning that light doesn't hit the retina (the lining at the back) in the right way. This can cause long-sightedness (where things close by are blurry), or short-sightedness (far away things are blurry - also called myopia). Not seeing clearly can lead to headaches, tiredness, and other problems.

WHAT CAUSES EYESIGHT PROBLEMS?

Like nearly everything, it's caused by a mixture of different things, including your DNA. Scientists also think that spending ages indoors, looking at things close to your face (toys, smartphones, even this book), can make myopia worse.

SO, WHAT CAN HELP PREVENT MYOPIA, OR STOP IT GETTING WORSE?

- ☑ Have regular eyesight tests.
- ☑ Wear glasses, if you need them.
- ☑ Take breaks from close up stuff, like homework (you still need to do it though – sorry!)
- ☑ Limit screentime (TVs, smartphones, that sort of thing).
- ☑ Spend lots of time outdoors! Go to the park, play sport, or take a walk in a forest.

WHY DO YOU HAVE TWO EARS?

Well, that's so you can tell where noise is coming from. Sounds hit one ear before the other and your brain works out where the sound is coming from. Clever, huh?

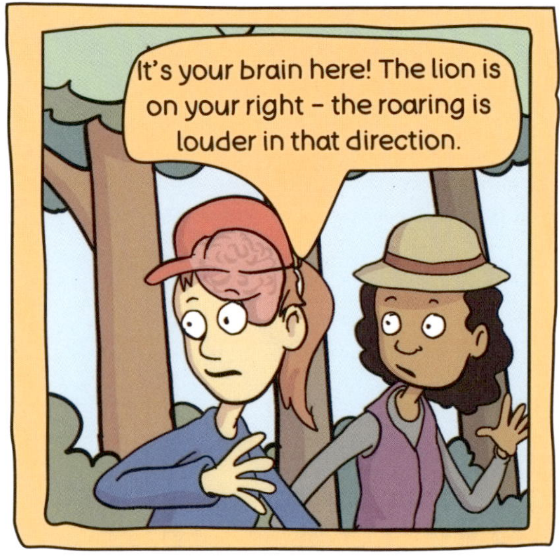

Humans are able to hear a whole range of sounds. This range is better than that of a chicken, but not as good as that of a cow, which can hear both higher and lower noises than us.

FUN FACT: YOUNG EARS

Children can usually hear sounds that are much higher-pitched than adults!

PARTS OF AN EAR

The outside part of each ear is made from cartilage, the tough, flexible substance we mentioned earlier. Don't worry about adding these to your human; you can pop these on later when you add the skin!

Your ears help to catch sounds which then travel inside your head, down your ear canal. This contains a special wax which helps protect the ear and fights off infections.

The sound reaches the ear drum, a thin piece of stretched skin. The ear drum vibrates. The louder the sound, the bigger the vibration. Three tiny bones in the middle ear then vibrate. The vibrations travel through the three bones to the cochlea, a tiny organ full of liquid.

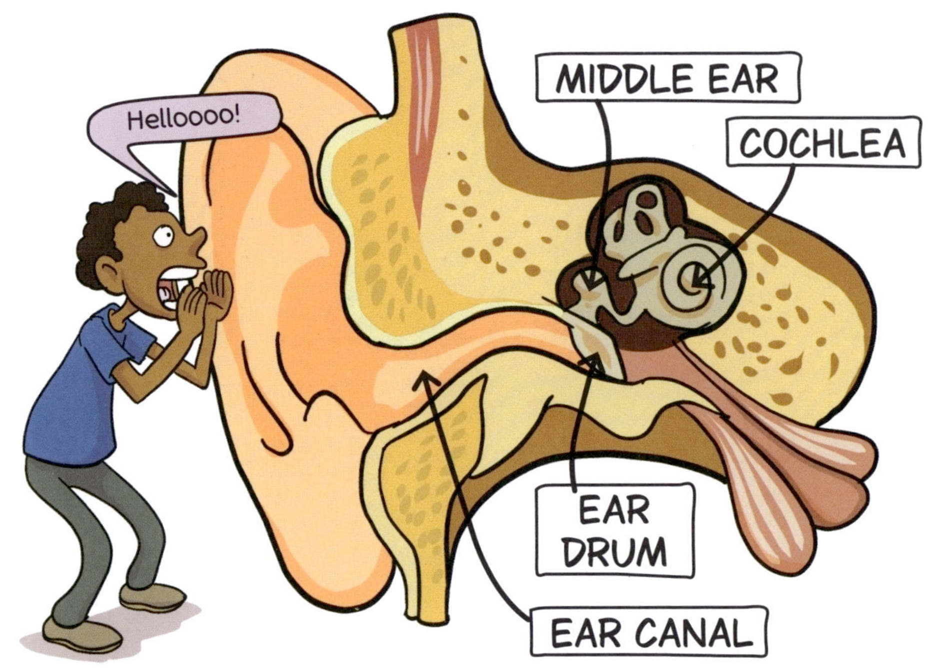

COCHLEA

The cochlea looks a bit like a snail shell. The vibrations make ripples in the fluid and tiny hairs detect this movement. They send signals to the brain through the cochlear nerve and your brain makes sense of it all. Incredible!

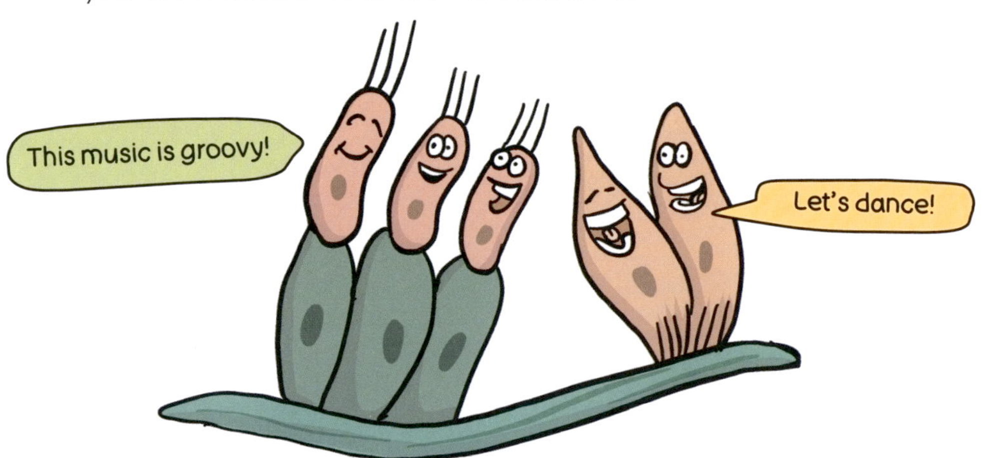

FUN FACT:

There's a little pocket of air in your middle ear. If you've ever been on an aeroplane, your ears may have "popped". That's because the air pressure inside has changed suddenly. They "pop" to make the pressure inside the ear the same as outside. Sniffing, yawning, or swallowing can all help to open the tubes that let air in and out.

ALL ABOUT NERVES

We'll cover the skin in detail later in the book (it'll be added last, otherwise you'll have a difficult job adding the inside bits!), but we can't mention senses and ignore touch. And that means talking about the nerves.

Your skin is covered in millions of nerves that detect different sensations. Nerves take these signals from all over the body to your brain. Not only that, but they are designed so that your body decides what to ignore and what to pay attention to, normally when something hurts.

LET'S LOOK AT HOW THAT WORKS:

Your feet notice when you first put on shoes but then ignore the sensation. Otherwise, you would have this happening all the time...

You're wearing shoes!
You're wearing shoes!
You're wearing shoes!

On other occasions, your body keeps going on and on and on, until you do something...

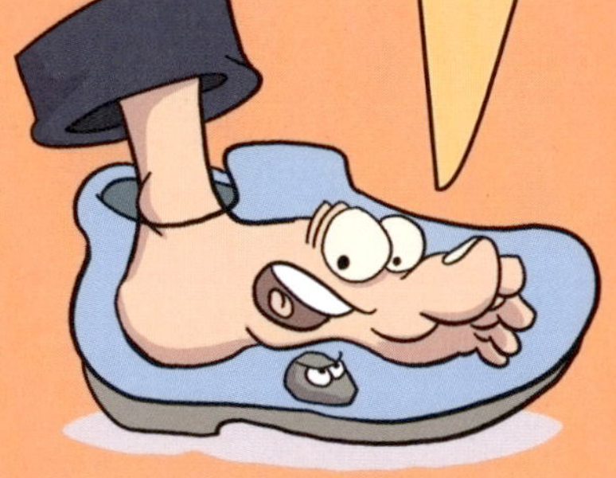

Some parts of your body have many more nerves than others. Also, different nerves do different things: they each detect certain sensations and ignore others.

NERVE ENDINGS

Free nerve endings help you to feel pain, as well as temperature and pressure changes. They wrap around the bottom of each individual hair, and can feel the wind, and even the lightest tough of something in your hair.

Nerve endings also feel texture and vibrations. There are some found deep in your skin that can detect stronger pressures, like tickling! Sensitive parts of your body, like your lips and the tips of your fingers, contain nerve endings that can detect the slightest touch too.

FUN FACT:

You cannot feel if something is wet. Wet things (like wet socks) often feel colder and heavier, and your brain sort of assumes they're wet, without really knowing for sure!

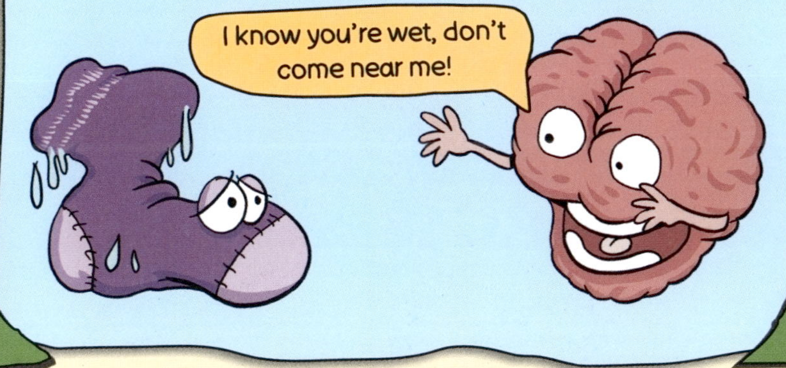

AND THE WINNER IS...

David Julius and **Ardem Patapoutian** received a **Nobel Prize in 2021** for their work on understanding how our bodies make sense of temperature and touch.

WHY DO YOU NEED TO SMELL?

Well, you don't. Just take a shower or a bath or put on some deodorant... ah... okay, I see what you mean. Right.

CAN YOU SMELL THAT?

Your sense of smell is very important. It can help you identify safe foods, is important in taste, and can help you identify danger. Your sense of smell helps answer important questions, such as, "Can I smell lion?" or, "Is something burning?" Particularly nasty odors can even make you sneeze.

HOW DOES SMELLING WORK?

You sniff, or breathe, and tiny particles race up your nose. At the top of your nose are cells with tiny hairs on them (similar to your cochlea). These hairs get excited by particular particles and send a signal to your brain if they detect them.

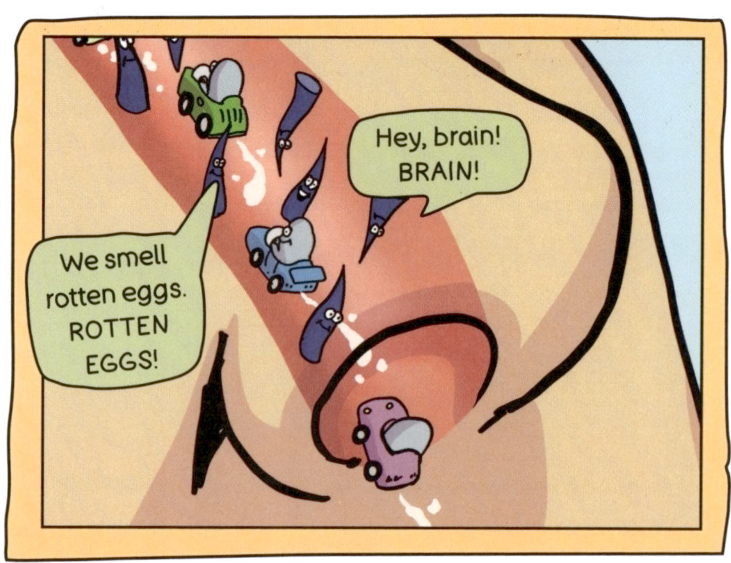

Many people think that our sense of smell is our least useful sense, but it's actually very important and interesting!

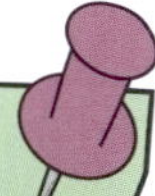

It's time for...

FOUR FACTS AND A FIB!

Can you spot the made-up fib lurking among the true facts?

1) Some scientists say we can detect as many as a trillion different smells.

2) Everyone has exactly the same sense of smell.

3) Most things make several smells: the smell of bananas is actually made from 300 different smell parts.

4) Scientists at the Chinese Academy of Science discovered that our sense of smell works incredibly quickly – faster than blinking our eyes!

5) People can follow the "trails" of some smells better than dogs!

Answer: Number 2 is a whopping fib! Not everyone smells the same stuff: some people cannot smell certain things, and what smells nice to you might smell horrible to someone else.

HOW TO SAFELY REMOVE A BOOGER

Boogers (or bogies) are lumps of dried mucus (the slimy stuff inside your nose). They can be very irritating, so it's no surprise that nose picking is very common. Most teenagers admit to doing it about four times a day! It's fairly harmless if you follow some simple rules:

1) Blow your nose first. This may dislodge the booger. Catch it in a paper tissue and throw it away. Wash your hands.

2) If nose picking is needed, find somewhere quiet, away from other people.

3) Make sure your nails are short as the inside of your nose is easily damaged. Wash your hands. You don't want nasty bacteria stuck up there!

4) Gently push some paper tissue in the nostril containing the booger. Hook it out. Throw both away. Do not eat the booger – it's a lump of dried mucus, remember? Wash your hands.

5) Do not make picking your nose a habit.

SO MUCH MUCUS

Our bodies make about one liter (a quarter of a gallon) of mucus each day, most of which we swallow – eww! Mucus helps the tiny hairs in our nostrils brush away annoying particles. Our bodies make more mucus when we have a virus, like a cold. Sneezing helps get rid of annoying bits and bobs – but remember to cover your nose when you sneeze!

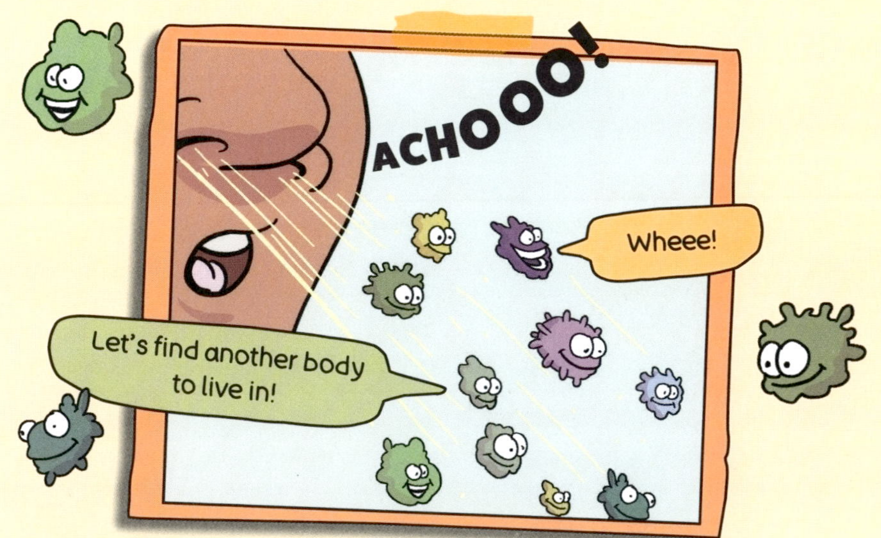

Rhinitis (righ-nigh-tus) is a common problem, especially among children. The inside of the nose becomes irritated, causing sneezing, itchiness, and a loss of smell. It's caused by all sorts of things: allergies, illnesses, changes in the weather, or a change in diet.

IF IT'S AN ALLERGY, IT'S IMPORTANT TO FIND WHAT IS CAUSING THE PROBLEM, WHICH COULD BE:

Medicines called antihistamines, nasal sprays, and salt water sprays can all help. So can washing cuddly toys and brushing pets. Being around dogs when you are very little may stop you getting rhinitis as badly.

HOW DOES TASTE WORK?

Taste helps you tell the difference between things that are good for you and things that are bad. This does not always work. Candy tastes good, but are not very good for you.

Your sense of taste works with your sense of smell. If you hold your nose and eat chocolate, it tastes different because your nose cannot smell the chocolate. If you have a cold, foods taste different because your nose is blocked.

Your tongue does the tasting. Chemicals in food are dissolved in your saliva (dribble) and your tongue recognizes the chemicals and tells your brain about them. The brain then decides what to do, such as...

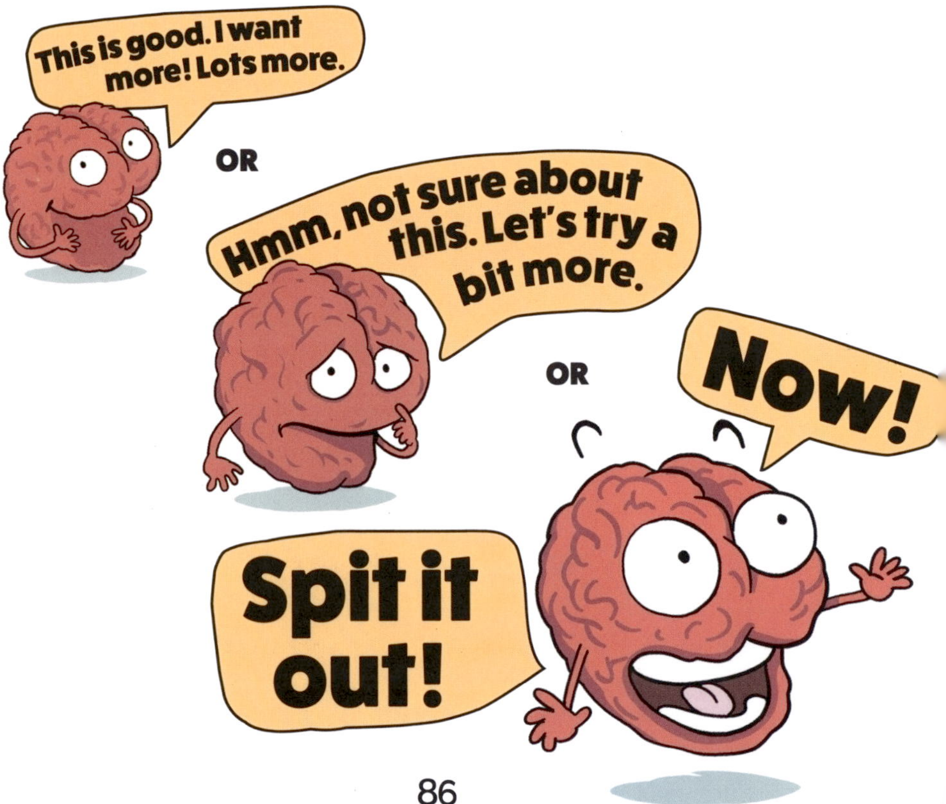

THERE ARE FIVE DIFFERENT TASTES:

TASTE:
Salty

FOUND IN:
Processed foods, potato chips, and jars of olives

MAKES YOU THINK:
This needs some salt or this is far too salty.

TASTE:
Sweet

FOUND IN:
Candy, fruit, and honey

MAKES YOU THINK:
Mmmmm, this is nice.

TASTE:
Sour

FOUND IN:
Lemons, rhubarb, and pickled foods

MAKES YOU THINK:
Hey, wait. Is this rotting?

TASTE:
Umami

FOUND IN:
Soy sauce, mature cheese, and cooked tomatoes

MAKES YOU THINK:
Do adults like this? I'm not sure I do.

TASTE:
Bitter

FOUND IN:
Coffee, dark chocolate, and cabbage

MAKES YOU THINK:
Is this poisonous?

Most foods are a mixture of different tastes. Some scientists think "fatty" could be a sixth taste. Metallic and watery may also be tastes.

Your tongue is covered in taste buds that detect the different tastes. You have thousands of these taste buds on your tongue especially at the sides, and more in other places in your mouth. Your tongue picks up other feelings too, including temperature and pain.

Clever tongue, working hard to keep you safe. Good tongue.

HOW MANY SENSES DO YOU HAVE?

Good question!

Here's a good answer.

There are the big five (sight, hearing, touch, smell, and taste) which tell you about the outside world. Thing is, scientists cannot agree even on that: some count touch as several senses because it tells you what's cold, what itches, and what tickles. Taste could be five senses (or more) rather than one.

OTHER SENSES TELL YOU ABOUT INSIDE YOUR BODY:

- **PROPRIOCEPTION** (pro-pri-o-sep-shun... try saying that ten times fast!) helps you understand where your body parts are. Can you put your left hand on your right elbow, or your nose, or your ear with your eyes closed? That's what we're talking about!
- Another sense helps you stay upright, tells you if you're speeding up, slowing down, spinning, or bending forward.
- Other senses tell you when you are hungry, thirsty, or need to go to the toilet.
- Your **HYPOTHALAMUS** (remember that?) keeps an eye on the time for you...

That's not all! You could have as many as 32 senses... or more.

COMMUNICATION

That's the senses more or less covered, but before we end the chapter, let's talk about some ways in which humans communicate. Humans have developed rich languages to share ideas and express feelings. This is only possible because of several different parts of our bodies.

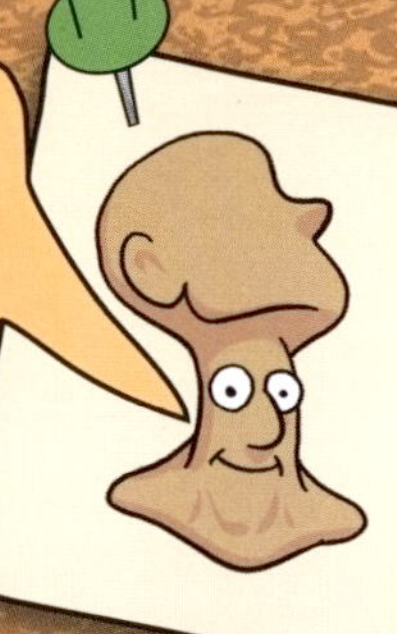

You communicate in other ways, too. You wave, frown, shrug, and smile and have different smiles to show different feelings.

HAPPY SMILE = I'M HAPPY

NERVOUS SMILE = I'M NERVOUS

EVIL SMILE = I HAVE A VILE PLAN TO CONQUER THE WORLD!

BLUSHING:

Blushing is where your face suddenly turns red because you are feeling shy, embarrassed, or proud. Scientists understand what causes your body to blush... but not why it wants to.

CRYING:

Crying is caused by many things: coughing, sadness, happiness, cutting up an onion... Glands above each eye make a liquid, and tear ducts (that's ducts, not ducks) near your nose help drain it away. Your body releases chemicals when you cry, meaning you'll often feel better afterwards. Crying also helps keep your eyes clean and healthy.

YAWNING:

When you yawn, your mouth opens wide, and you take a deep breath. You may yawn to cool down your brain but, like many things, why we yawn is still a mystery. Yawning is also contagious: others can catch it, even different types of animal! When one person (or cat, or whatever) yawns, others often copy them. Perhaps it's a way of saying to others that it's time to have a snooze.

Feeling sleepy yet?

Chapter 5:

LET'S PLUG IN THE HEART!

NEXT, IT'S TIME TO ADD THE HEART

The heart is heart shaped, but not in the way you think it is. It also has little to do with who you love or why you love them. Your heart is a muscle – a pump sending thousands of liters (over a thousand gallons) of blood* around your body every day.

*It's the same blood, going around and around. A 10-year-old human has about 2.5 liters (0.66 gallons) in their body.

Your blood delivers essential oxygen and nutrients to every cell, helps deliver messages, and helps you heal. Without your heart, the rest of your body would quickly stop working and your cells would begin to die.

Your heart is about the size of your fist. It sits in the middle of your chest, pointing slightly to the left, and is one of the organs protected by your ribcage.

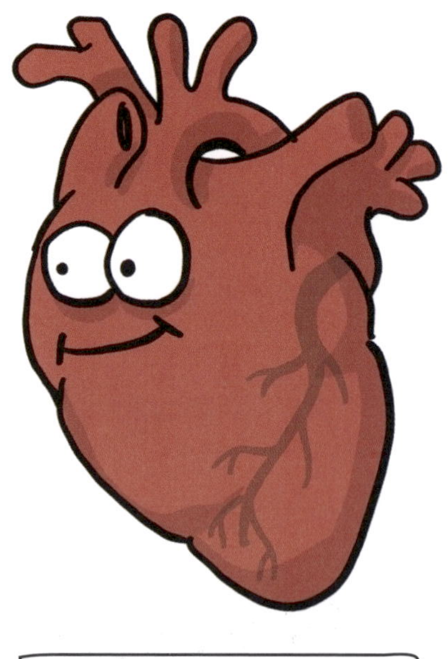

... BUT THIS SHAPE!

WAIT, HOW MANY?

Your heart beats about 80 times a minute, which is more than 100,000 times a day. That's over 40 million times each year!

I think you'd agree: that's a lot of beats. Your heart has to keep a nice steady rhythm, day in, day out... and night in, night out too. It has to speed up when you exercise, and slow down when you rest. So, it's no wonder that sometimes things go wrong.

However, those hard-working scientists are on the case, searching for solutions to heart disease.

Let's take a look at some of the things they've been up to:

BREAKTHROUGH:
AI

USED FOR:
Predicting heart attacks

TELL ME MORE!
AI has one huge advantage over doctors: it's incredibly fast. AI can "look" at X-rays and computer images of patients' hearts and predict how likely they are to have a heart attack. It can then, with supervision from human doctors, recommend changes in lifestyle to help stop this happening!

BREAKTHROUGH:
3D printing

USED FOR:
Creating tiny blood vessels

TELL ME MORE!
Working together, scientists from the University of Strathclyde in the UK and Tsinghua University in China have 3D printed tiny tubes that can carry blood. These could be used to test new medicines (meaning that animals would not have to be used anymore) and could also help grow entire organs in labs that could be used in transplants*.

*An organ transplant happens when a patient's organ, such as their heart, no longer works properly and needs to be replaced.

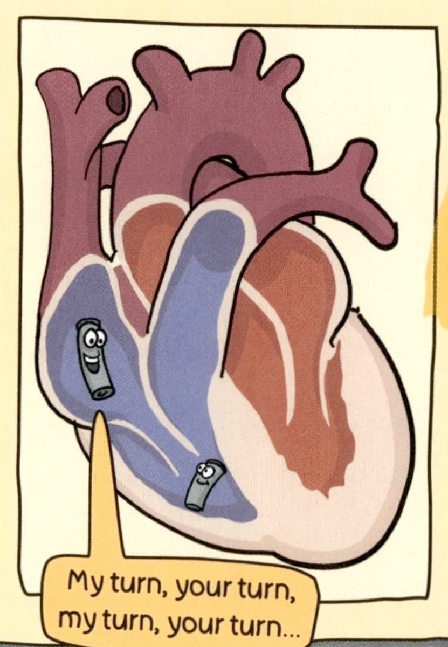

BREAKTHROUGH:
Wireless pacemakers

USED FOR:
Keeping the heart beating

TELL ME MORE!
Pacemakers help patients' hearts keep regular beats. They are usually wired into a patient's heart and use tiny pulses of electricity to make the heart contract. New pacemakers are implanted straight into the heart in pairs and "talk" with each other wirelessly!

BREAKTHROUGH:
Stem cell patches

USED FOR:
Repairing damaged hearts

TELL ME MORE!
Small patches of heart cells are grown by scientists in the lab using stem cells. These are then stitched onto hearts to replace damaged parts.

YOUR HEART WORKS INCREDIBLY HARD...

...and so it needs more oxygen than any other muscle. When you exercise, your heart beats faster because your other muscles and organs need more oxygen than usual.

Your heart is made from four chambers, like tiny rooms, called atriums and ventricles. The upstairs atriums beat a fraction of a second before the downstairs ventricles. Blood coming from around your body enters the right side of your heart and is then sent to your lungs. Oxygen-rich blood from the lungs comes back into the left side.

Your heartbeat causes your pulse, which is like a wave of blood through your body. By pressing the first two fingers of either hand against certain places in your body you can find your pulse (don't use your thumb - it has a pulse of its own).

You can try pressing your fingers gently against the inside of your wrist or the side of your neck. Don't panic if you can't find your pulse. It can be hard to locate...

HOW EXACTLY DOES YOUR HEART BEAT?

Inside your heart is a patch of nerve cells. This uses a tiny pulse of electricity to control your heartbeat without any interference from your brain. However, your brain still needs to tell your heart to slow down or speed up, depending on what you're making your body do.

Arteries are tubes that take oxygen-rich blood away from the heart. These have to be thick and tough because the heart pushes blood down them at great pressure.

Veins collect and bring blood back to your heart. They use valves (like doors that only open one way) to make sure that blood flows in one direction only.

Capillaries are vessels that grow up to become butterflies (...sorry, sorry, that's caterpillars – please ignore). Capillaries (not caterpillars) are tiny. They are just wide enough for one cell to travel down. They take the blood exactly where it is needed, and then take it away again!

In your body, there are thousands of miles of blood vessels. If they were put in one long line, they could wrap around the world twice!

SO, WHAT EXACTLY IS BLOOD?

An adult human has about 5 liters (1.3 gallons) of blood. You might have about half of that, depending on how big and old you are. Just over half of blood is made of a pale-yellow liquid called plasma.

On its own, plasma looks a lot like pee. It is mostly water, but there are also many useful things mixed into it, including...

1. **GLUCOSE** (a type of sugar)
2. **INGREDIENTS** for making proteins
3. **IRON**
4. **VITAMINS**
5. **A SPECIAL PROTEIN** that helps your blood clot, meaning bleeding stops

There are also billions of special cells and cell-like things in your blood. Just one drop of your blood contains:

1. **15 MILLION PLATELETS**
2. **500,000 WHITE BLOOD CELLS**
3. **250 MILLION RED BLOOD CELLS**

We'll take a good look at what these do in the next few pages. Red blood cells have tiny markers on them to tell your white blood cells that they belong to your body.

These markers give you your blood group. There are different types of blood groups, including “A”, “B”, “AB”, and “O”. It’s important to know blood groups for things like transfusion, where blood is taken from one person and given to another who needs it. Group “A” blood cannot be given to somebody with group “B” blood. Most people belong to blood group “O”, which has no markers. This means that group “O” blood can be safely given to anybody else who needs a transfusion.

WHAT ELSE IS IN YOUR BLOOD?

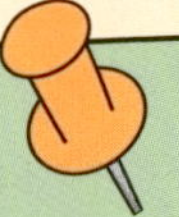

Let’s take a look at red blood cells, using...

FOUR FACTS AND A FIB!

Can you spot the made-up fib lurking among the true facts?

1) Red blood cells are definitely cells.

2) They’re the most common cells in your body — about 85% of your cells are red blood cells. That’s 17 out of every 20 cells, or 25 trillion in your whole body!

3) Red blood cells travel through blood vessels. In your capillaries, they squeeze through one by one, giving life-giving oxygen to other cells who need it.

4) Every second, your body makes 2 million new red blood cells in your bone marrow.

5) Red blood cells don’t last long. After about three or four months, they die. Special white blood cells then gobble them up. The stuff inside is recycled to make new blood cells.!

Answer: Number 1 could be a fib! Many scientists don’t think they’re cells because grown-up red blood cells don’t have a nucleus (tiny recipe-library) inside them, and they cannot create copies of themselves.

SO, WHAT DO THEY LOOK LIKE?

Red blood not-cells (see what I did there?) have an interesting shape. They are "squished" in the middle (a bit like that time I gripped my chocolate muffin too hard), which gives them a larger surface area to carry oxygen.

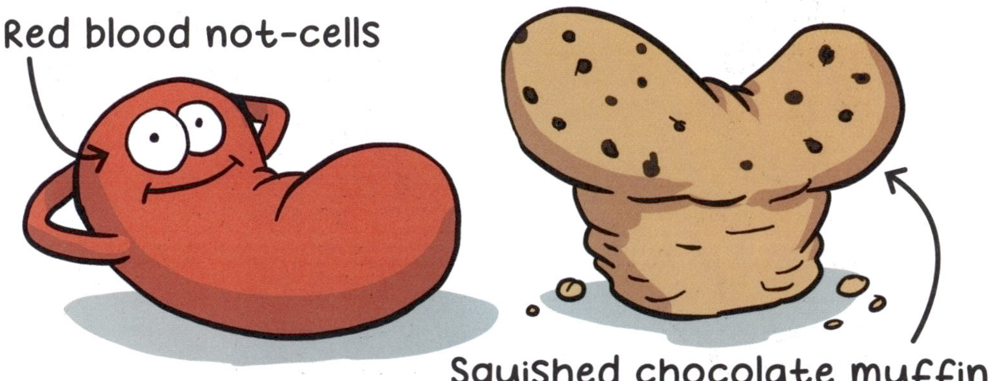

This shape also makes them flexible, allowing them to move down narrow blood vessels.

The job of red blood not-cells is to collect oxygen from the lungs and take it all around your body. They also take away waste (like carbon dioxide). Every red blood not-cell is stuffed full of a protein called haemoglobin, about 300 million bits of it! When haemoglobin mixes with oxygen, it turns bright red, which gives blood its color. Haemoglobin also contains tiny amounts of iron, which is why blood has a metallic taste.*

*It's probably okay to taste your own blood. Animals lick their wounds because mouth saliva helps to heal the wound. However, your mouth also contains lots of bacteria (about 600 different types in fact), so it's probably better to wash the wound with clean water instead. What's NOT okay is tasting other people's blood. That's just weird. You are not a vampire.

IN THE PARK...
Should I lick it?
Did someone say... BLOOD?!
I'll taste it for you!
Foul!
Mouths are full of bacteria, and you, Count Cringeula, are waaay out of line!
Much better!
Being healthy is no fun...

WHAT EXACTLY IS A PLATELET?

Well, if a baby eagle is an eaglet and a baby owl is an owlet, is a baby plate a platelet? **NO, IT ISN'T.**

Platelets are tiny plate-shaped structures much smaller than red blood cells (I've given up calling them not-cells). Platelets are DEFINITELY NOT cells, though they are made in the same places as red blood cells.

They are instead pieces of cells. Or maybe cell-lets? Cell-lings?

1 You make about a million new platelets every second. They travel around in the blood with one job in mind: sealing wounds.

2 Once they get the signal, they travel to the damaged blood vessel. First, they tell the vein or artery to contract (to stop more blood from being wasted). Then, each platelet grows tiny tentacles that stick to other platelets and the sides of the damaged blood vessel. At this point, they no longer look like plates, but instead resemble a weird alien life-form, or the sort of thing you would find living at the bottom of the ocean.

3 They then work with a protein in your plasma to make a jelly-like substance that closes the wound. This dries to make a scab.

4 Once they're done, the blood vessel opens up again. Your platelets send out more signals to say they have finished, and other cells get to work, eating up any nasty stuff and making a more permanent repair.

Platelets have a very important role to play, but they do not have long to live. After a week or so, they die.

MEANWHILE, INSIDE A BLOOD VESSEL...
MISSION ALERT!
Come in Artery, you need to contract
Artery received, contracting now!
SUPERHERO TRANSFORMATION...
The scab has been placed!

WHAT ARE WHITE BLOOD CELLS?

White blood cells are a really important part of the body's immune system. They deal with any nasties that do not belong. like tiny microbes including bacteria or viruses.

HOW DO WHITE BLOOD CELLS KNOW WHAT TO DO?

Well, your blood contains special proteins called antibodies. These travel around in your plasma and work in different ways.

SOME ANTIBODIES...

1. stick to a nasty and tell your white blood cells to devour it
2. surround the nasty, stopping it from attacking
3. glue nasties together to slow down infection

Antibodies only notice one type of nasty (e.g. the chickenpox or varicella virus) and ignore all others. Luckily, your body produces about 10 billion different antibodies, one for each type of nasty (yep, there are a lot of nasties out there!)

White blood cells also gobble up other damaged or dead cells.

White blood cells travel around in your blood and in the lymphatic system. This is a network of tiny tubes that works alongside your blood vessels. Bean-shaped lymph nodes provide tiny waiting rooms for your white blood cells; a place to hang out when they are not needed.

Let's meet some of the heroic little cells that keep you safe and healthy.

"I'm a neutrophil. Call me Phil. I'm pretty common, but I'm fast and I'm always first on the scene. I chase nasties and take 'em out! I only live for a couple of days but it's an exciting existence. Ever had icky white pus in a wound? Or a spot? That's made from dead cells just like me!"

"I'm a monocyte. Call me Mo. I'm pretty big but I can move through your tissues looking for nasties. My job is to gobble one up and find out exactly what type of nasty it is. I then pass this information on to my mates, the lymphocytes. I can eat about 100 nasties before life gets too much... and I die."

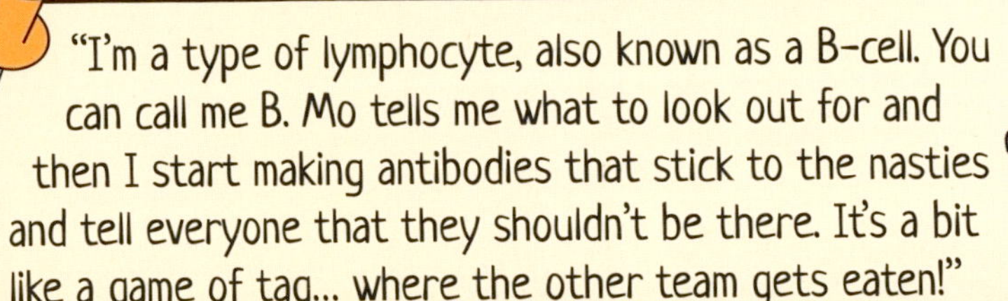

"I'm a type of lymphocyte, also known as a B-cell. You can call me B. Mo tells me what to look out for and then I start making antibodies that stick to the nasties and tell everyone that they shouldn't be there. It's a bit like a game of tag... where the other team gets eaten!"

"I'm a different type of lymphocyte, also known as a T-cell. You can call me T. I sometimes make more B-cells or I might go after stuff that B has tagged. Once I catch a nasty, I spray it with deadly antibodies. Once I'm activated, there's no stopping me."

Some of your lymphocytes become memory cells. These hang around in your body for years and have one job: remember how to destroy a particular type of nasty. They might remember how to fight chickenpox, or measles, or even a cold virus, stopping you from getting the same virus again.

OH NO, I FEEL FAINT!

Your blood pressure is a measure of how hard your heart is pushing against your arteries, the tubes that carry blood away from your heart.

It needs to be high enough so that your blood keeps moving but not so high that your arteries are put under strain. Older people often have higher blood pressure because their arteries are stiffer and less stretchy, and babies and young children have lower blood pressure because they are small.

Low blood pressure can be a problem because the muscles and organs are not getting enough oxygen. This can cause dizziness, blurred vision, and fainting. Low blood pressure can be caused by drugs, lack of water, or even from standing up too long. On the other hand, high blood pressure can cause problems with sleep and vision, as well as more serious problems. It can be caused by stress, lack or exercise, or eating too much salt.

Luckily, your body is incredibly good at trying to keep everything running smoothly. To keep your blood pressure at a good level, it helps to get regular exercise and eat a healthy, balanced diet.

Okay, that's enough about the heart. Let's move on to your other organs.

Chapter 6:

ORGANISING THE OTHER ORGANS

Now that your human has a skeleton, a brain, senses, and a heart. It's time to add

THE OTHER ORGANS.

This chapter is stuffed full of organs. Any of them could have had a chapter of their own, but there's just not enough space, so they only get a couple of pages each… if they're lucky.

Sorry, spleen.

But make no mistake: all of these organs have their own role to play in keeping you alive. Some of them are just as important as the brain or the heart. You would not survive without them, or not for long anyway. Some of them, well… let's just say they're kind of there and it's nice to have them, but if they went missing, you probably wouldn't notice.

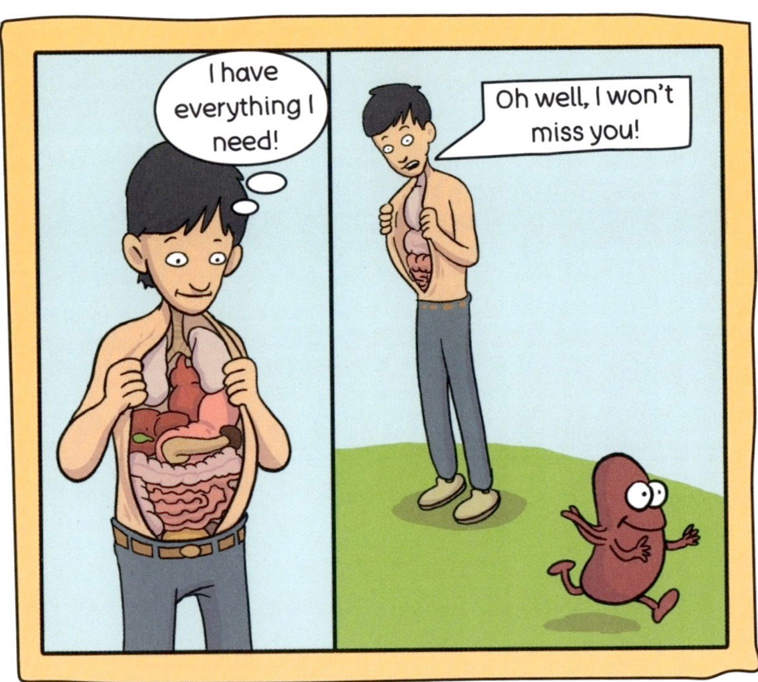

Sorry again, spleen. But sometimes, the truth hurts.

Your body is complex. You have lots of different organs, each with its own job (or jobs) and these organs "talk" to each other to say how they're getting on and whether there's anything they need.

There are, of course, things that can go wrong, so scientists are kept busy thinking up new techniques and technology to solve problems.

Let's take a look at some:

BREAKTHROUGH:
Lab-grown organs used for replacing failed organs

TELL ME MORE!
Organ transplants have been around for a long time. These rely on organ donations, with drugs* being used to stop patient's bodies rejecting these new organs. However, 3D printing and stem cell techniques could mean new organs are grown or made, possibly even using a patient's own stem cells. That would mean no organ-rejecting drugs any more.

*Organ rejection happens because the body's immune system does not "recognize" the organ and so attacks it. Gertrude Elion and George Hitchings developed the first drug that stopped organ rejection and received a Nobel Prize in 1988!

BREAKTHROUGH:

Organs-on-chips used for creating tiny versions of organs

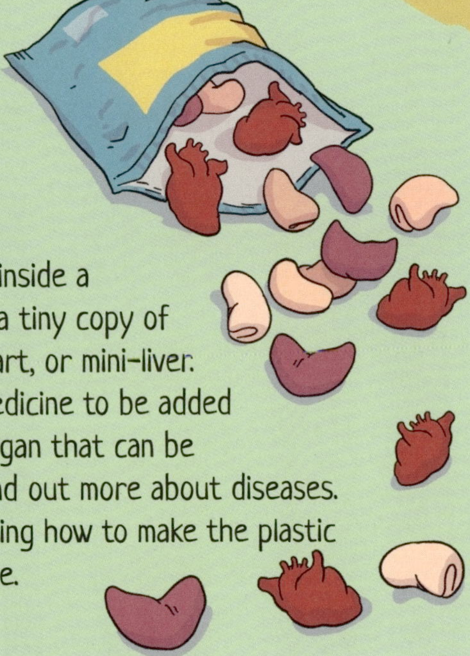

TELL ME MORE!

A few human cells are grown inside a small plastic chip and act like a tiny copy of an organ: a mini-lung, mini-heart, or mini-liver. Little channels allow air or medicine to be added and... you've got a working organ that can be used to test new drugs or find out more about diseases. Scientists are even investigating how to make the plastic chip sustainable and recyclable.

BREAKTHROUGH:

Gene scissors used for rewriting our DNA

TELL ME MORE!

Some people are born with a disease: it's written in their DNA. Scientists are developing techniques that find the part of the code that gives a patient a dangerous condition and "snip" it out. They hope to be able to cure many different diseases using this technique.*

* Emmanuelle Charpentier and Jennifer A. Doudna received a Nobel Prize in Chemistry in 2020 for their work on gene scissors.

So, what about all those other organs?
Let's start with **YOUR LUNGS.**

Let's take a look at how the lungs work.

1) Your lungs expand because the muscles in your ribcage move, including a very important one called the diaphragm.

2) A mixture of gases, germs, dust, and other stuff is pulled into your body. The tiny hairs in your nose – if you breathe through your nose – catch some of the nasties in their sticky mucus.

3) The air passes down your windpipe. Some goes into your left lung and some into your right, passing into smaller and smaller tubes until it reaches tiny inflatable alveoli. These are hundreds of millions of miniscule balloons in your lungs.

4) The oxygen passes through the walls of these balloons, which are just one cell thick. Meanwhile, carbon dioxide passes out the other way. The oxygen enters your blood vessels.

5) You breathe out, getting rid of the poisonous carbon dioxide that your body does not want. You breathe faster if you're exercising, to take in all the extra oxygen your muscles need.

6) Repeat: in out, in out – about 20 times a minute. That's nearly 30,000 times a day, or about 10 million breaths every year.

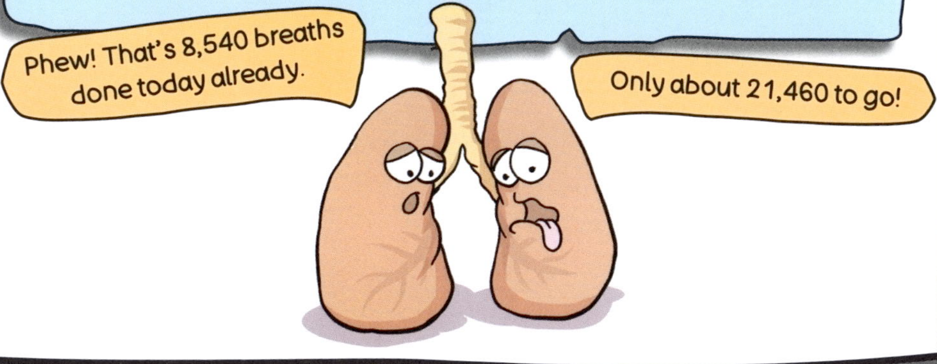

Phew! That's 8,540 breaths done today already.

Only about 21,460 to go!

FUN FACT:

Your lungs have a huge surface area, meaning that your body can absorb lots of oxygen with every breath. If you were to spread a set of lungs flat (do NOT try this out) they would cover an area of 260 square meters (2,800 square feet) – about the same as a tennis court!

LET'S MOVE ONTO THE LIVER

Or, as I think of it, *The Wonder Organ*.

An adult human liver weighs about 1.5 kg (3.3 lbs), making it the largest internal organ. It has a long list of jobs: it's almost as though when the jobs were given out, the liver volunteered for nearly all of them...

Okay, organs. Time to sort out those jobs. So, who'd like to make glucose? And we'll need someone to make blood-clotting proteins. Oh, and who wants to make bile? It helps our body digest fat.

Oh, I'll do that! All of those. No problem.

Great, thanks Liver. So next, we need someone to make hormones that'll help make platelets, grow cells, and control blood pressure? Oh, and then we need someone to sort through nutrients from the intestines, and store vitamins and minerals, like iron and copper?

Me! Me! Pick me! I can do it.

Impressive. Okay, and who is going to clean the blood, destroy old blood cells, and kill bacteria? Who is going to deal with the really nasty chemicals, poisons - that sort of thing? Anybody else?

...Guess I could take that on too? Why not!

Your liver does all of these things and... it can also regenerate itself! A human liver may have to deal with all sorts of nasty stuff (like poisons) which can cause a lot of damage. If it is badly injured, the liver can actually regrow most of itself. Brilliant, huh?

The liver also has its own private security force. Kupffer cells cling to the sides of the blood vessels and pounce on any nasties or old, tired cells, and devour them!

FUN FACT:

Your pee is yellow because of a chemical the liver uses when it takes apart old blood cells.

Food gives you energy to move and keeps your cells alive. And learning to cook food may have given humans our unusually large brains. Cooking means that our bodies can break down and make use of all the good stuff in food more easily. If we did not cook, we'd have to spend either more time eating or shrink the size of our brains. That doesn't mean that all food needs to be cooked: raw food, such as apples, are very healthy.

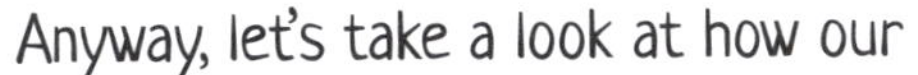

DIGESTIVE SYSTEM WORKS.

Your digestive system is all the organs involved in eating — and yep, there's a lot of them!

HOW DO WE DIGEST A SNACK?

"It's Friday, it's 5 o'clock, and you're joining me in Sam's body. And it looks like stomach is empty. Yes, that's right... it's telling hypothalamus that Sam needs food."

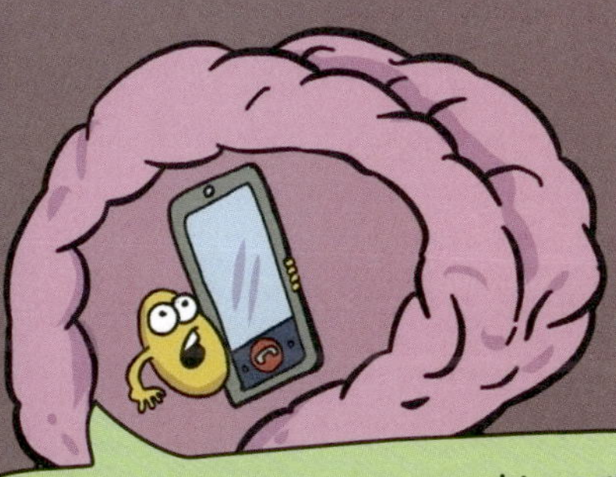

Look Sam, I think we need to eat, the stomach is making such a fuss!

"And look! An apple! Sam's eyes are telling brain, and brain is telling mouth to start making saliva. Sam's beginning to dribble. What will he do? It's nearly dinner time and... HE'S TAKEN THE APPLE! Did you see that! His arm shot out and grabbed it!"

“Now Sam’s teeth are going to work, taking a bite, and grinding the apple to a pulp. Saliva is joining in, using a protein to help break down the food. Taste buds on Sam’s tongue are now working and... they’re telling brain that Sam is in fact eating an apple! The food is safe!”

“Tongue is tossing the bits of apple around, squashing it, then pushing it to the back and... throat swallows! Goal!”

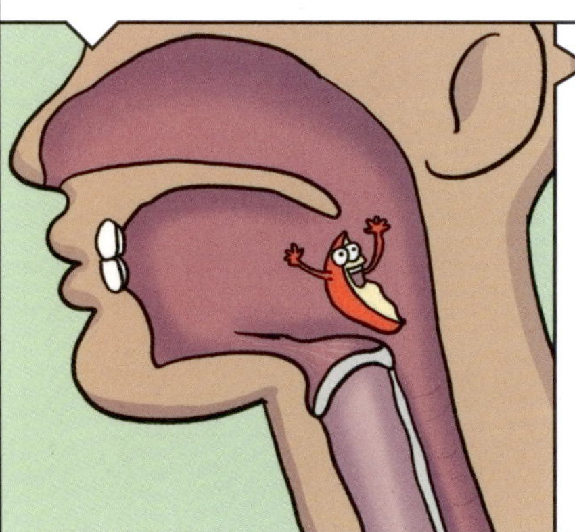

“Epiglottis* seals the windpipe and the lump of apple goes down, pushed and helped along by muscles, until it reaches Sam’s stomach. The real process of digestion is about to begin!”

*Your epiglottis is a flap protecting your lungs.

OK, LET’S TAKE A BREAK

Your digestive system has the job of breaking down food into the smallest possible parts, then sending these to other parts of the body. There are three main organs: the stomach, the small intestine (which is about 6 meters, or 20 ft, long), and the large intestine (which is 1.5 meters, or 5 ft, short).

THERE ARE DIFFERENT CELLS IN YOUR DIGESTIVE SYSTEM.

1) Some stomach cells produce acids that break down food.

2) Cells in your intestines use tiny fingers to absorb useful nutrients.

3) Goblet cells make mucus to help protect the other cells. Without this mucus, your stomach acid would enter your body... and start digesting it! Eeek!

4) Some cells send messages to the brain when your stomach is full.

LET'S GET BACK TO THE ACTION!

"And Sam's stomach gets to work quickly, producing acid and proteins to break down the apple. More chewed-up apple arrives and stomach slowly turns it into a disgusting soup, ready for small intestine. Stomach's also busy absorbing water from the apple, which it sends to liver."

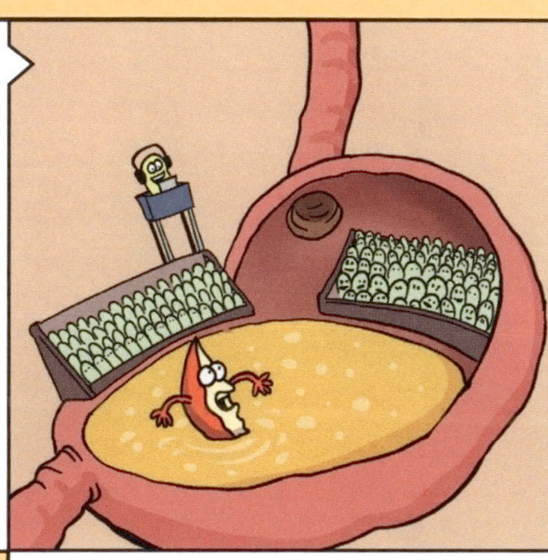

SEVERAL HOURS LATER

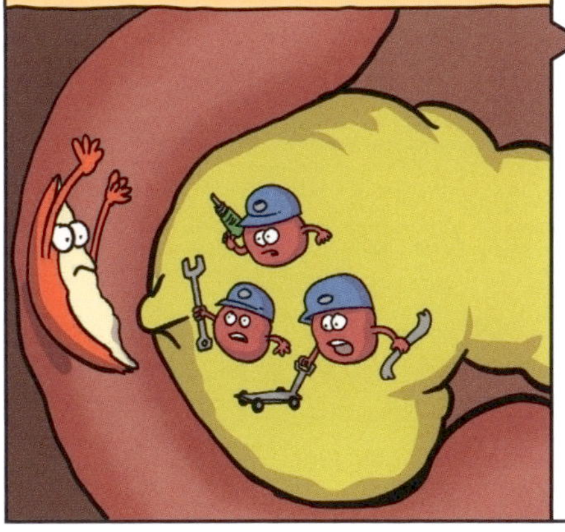

"I believe stomach has begun sending the acidic apple soup to small intestine. Yes, there it goes! And pancreas is getting stuck in, sending digestive proteins into small intestine. And here's liver, sending over bile. Things don't look good for apple... and there's still about 6 meters (nearly 20 ft) of this to go!

"The apple is slowly being absorbed as it moves through small intestine... more and more is being grabbed by the tiny finger-like villi on each cell. I can see the carbohydrates being taken; even the tiny amount of protein and fat are not wasted. I don't think the apple can come back from here."

ABOUT A DAY LATER...

"It's day two, and I think we can agree: it's all over for apple. It's now reached Sam's large intestine. I have to say, it looks nothing like an apple anymore. Most of the good stuff's already taken, but the large intestine is still trying to grab any vitamins or minerals lurking in the mush."

"And here come the gut bacteria! Trillions of tiny microbes have descended on the remains of the apple, helping to break it down. And slowly, the apple is squeezed along towards...

Well, I think we'll leave it there! Thanks for listening, and join me tomorrow when... Sam eats a banana!"

THE END, FOR NOW...

FUN FACT:

Food can spend up to a day in your large intestine. Here, trillions of helpful bacteria and other microbes do incredible work breaking down food, killing nasty bacteria, and producing useful vitamin K. They even give your poo its brown color! In fact, up to one-third of your poo is made of these friendly microbes.

By the time your food nears the end of its journey, your large intestine will have removed as much useful stuff as it can. The large intestine releases mucus to keep it moist and help stick it together, then stores it in the rectum (a sort of waiting room for poo).

As more and more poo collects, the rectum stretches slightly, signaling the brain that it's time to find a toilet!

The poo is pushed out through an opening called the anus. This is often accompanied by gases made by your gut bacteria. This may make interesting sounds and funky smells! These smells are released at other times too, whenever there's a build-up of gases that can no longer be contained by your body.

LET'S LEAVE POO BEHIND... AND TALK ABOUT PEE INSTEAD!

Your cells take energy from the food you eat, but they also make waste products: carbon dioxide, harmful chemicals, and toxins (poisonous stuff). This waste travels around in your blood.

That's where your **kidneys** come in!

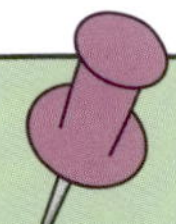

FOUR FACTS AND A FIB!

Can you spot the made-up fib lurking among the true facts?

1) You have two kidneys at the bottom of your ribcage, either side of your back. They are the same shape as kidney beans. Or maybe kidney beans are the same shape as kidneys... hmmm?

2) They clean your blood. They leave red and white blood cells and proteins alone, but separate everything else. Your clever kidneys then release useful stuff back into the blood, making sure you don't have too much of anything.

3) They help keep your blood pressure steady and help your body use calcium.

4) Your kidneys collect urine. This watery liquid contains things your body does not want: salts, acids, and a waste product called urea.

5) Your kidneys are grown by your knees before you are born.

Answer: Number 5 is a whopping lie. They are kidneys, not kid-knees.

Your kidneys drain the urine (or pee) into your bladder. This is a stretchy sack below your hips. An adult bladder can hold about half a liter (1 pt) of liquid. When it is full, the nerve cells inside signal the brain.

When you are ready, muscles around your bladder contract, the urine passes down a tube called the urethra and then leaves your body.

How much urine you produce depends on how much liquid you drink. Fresh urine is clean enough to drink but this should only be done in the most desperate situations. Your pee contains lots of things your body wants to get rid of.

Why do we have two kidneys? Because then it doesn't matter if one stops working (we can live happily with just one). So why don't we have two hearts, or two brains? Maybe it's simply because kidneys use much less energy than certain other organs, and argue less.

SOME ORGANS YOU CANNOT LIVE WITHOUT. SOME YOU CAN. LET'S MEET THEM.

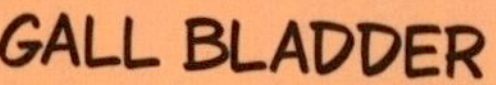

"Hi there, I'm gall bladder. I'm a muscular bag used to store bile, a liquid made by liver. Bile is particularly good at breaking down hard-to-digest fat. I can suffer from gallstones, which are made when a type of fat hardens into a small hard rock inside me. If you're fairly careful about what you eat, you can live without me."

APPENDIX

"I'm appendix, a finger-shaped (and finger-sized) organ near your large intestine. For a long time, scientists thought I was completely useless, but I may have helped your distant ancestors digest plants. Some scientists now believe helpful bacteria hang out inside me and I may play a part in helping your body fight infection. I can suffer from appendicitis, which is when I become swollen. You can have me removed and live a perfectly normal life."

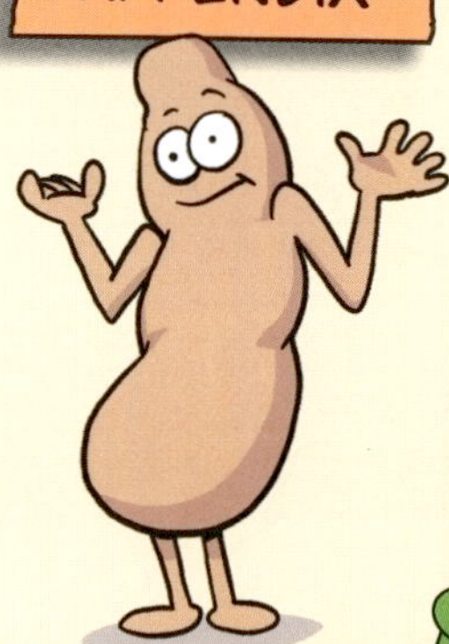

TONSILS

"Hey there, we're your tonsils! You'll find us the back and either side of your mouth. we're only little but we help your immune system fight infection. We suffer from tonsillitis which is when we become swollen and painful. If this keeps happening, doctors may decide to remove us. It's quite common and people who've had an operation are happy afterwards. Happier, in fact, as they don't keep getting sore throats!"

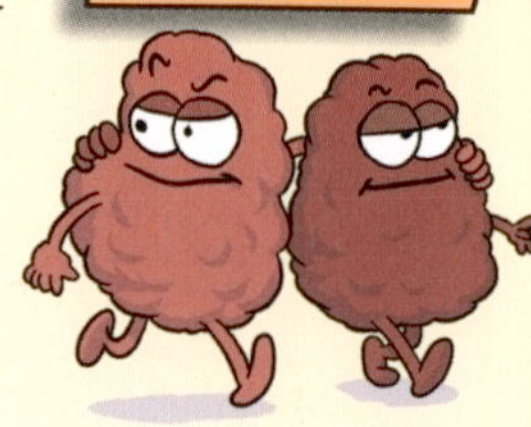

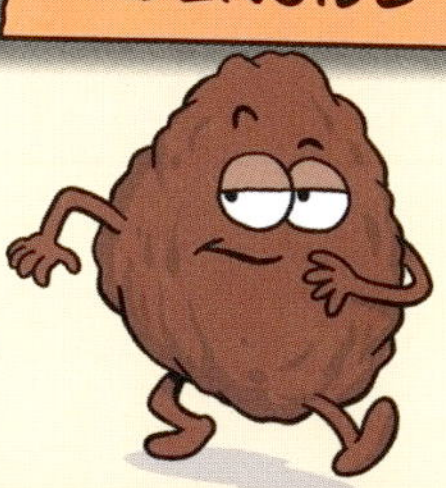

"Hi! It's me, your tiny adenoids. I'm also part of your immune system and I'm found where your nose passages meet your mouth. Just like the tonsils, I can become infected and swollen and may need to be removed (sorry about that). But it's okay, because you can live without me. Hooray!"

THYMUS GLAND

"Yo. Thymus gland here. I make and train highly skilled white blood cells. These fight infection in your body, like mini ninja warriors. By the time you become a teenager, my work is finished. When you become an adult, I start to shrink. Your body no longer has need of me. If I must be removed, then... so be it."

SPLEEN

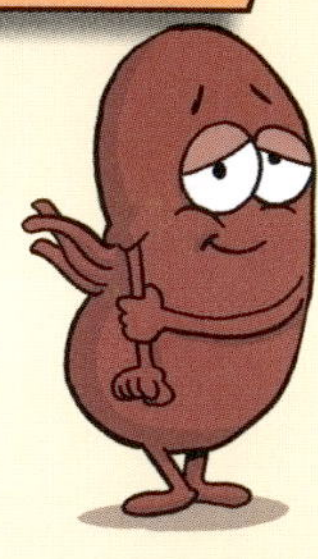

"Hello. I'm spleen. I'm part of your immune system. I sit below your heart and I'm about the shape and size of your fist. I clean the blood, and remove old blood cells and other nasty stuff. Sometimes, I get a tiny, weeny bit excited by my job and start taking out healthy cells or platelets. Know what that means? Yep, it's time for little old me to be taken out!"

Some people are born without a spleen and some people have two, one of which is usually much smaller. Doctors are reluctant to take out spleens because it can leave patients more likely to get infections...

Chapter 7:

THE FINISHING TOUCHES

Hopefully, you've added all the important inside body bits and connected everything up.

NOW IT'S TIME TO ADD THE SKIN!

Your body is covered in skin. You probably knew that. But do you realise how incredible skin is?

Skin is tough, flexible, and stretchy. It's waterproof and protects you from all sorts of nasties. It's able to tell the difference between something sharp, something cold, and something tickly. It keeps you cool (or warm), and helps you stay healthy by producing vitamin D from sunlight.

Your skin is your largest organ. The average adult human has 10 kg (22 lb) of skin altogether, about the same mass as a bowling ball or two pet cats. If it was stretched out (do NOT do this) it would cover two square meters (21 square feet).

THE TRULY AMAZING THING?

Your body grows a whole new layer of outer skin every month.

CAN WE HELP THE SKIN?

Skin is amazing, but it comes under constant attack every day. It repels bacteria, viruses, and fungi, while being battered by sunlight and scraped, scratched, and bruised. Poor skin! As a living organ, the skin does a brilliant job of dealing with this, but sometimes it needs a bit of extra help.

That's where clever scientists come in! Let's take a look at some of the developing science that is being used...

BREAKTHROUGH:
Helpful bacteria used for getting rid of smelly bacteria

TELL ME MORE!
Your skin is covered with millions of tiny microbes, including many that keep skin healthy. And it's not actually you that smells when you sweat, but the bacteria that live on your skin. A study using identical twins showed that bacteria scraped from the armpit of one twin (who smelt nice) and put into the armpit of the other (who had a funkier smell) can help solve these body odor problems for several weeks!

BREAKTHROUGH:
3D printing used for replacing damaged skin

TELL ME MORE!
Scientists are developing 3D printed skin using living cells that could help with healing or replace damaged areas of skin. A patient's own stem cells* could be used, meaning their body should not reject the new patches of skin.

*Stem cells can develop into different cells. This process can also be reversed, and a "grown-up cell" (such as a skin cell) can be turned back into a stem cell. Shinya Yamanaka and Sir John Gurdon were awarded a Nobel Prize in 2012 because of this amazing discovery!

BREAKTHROUGH:
Skin regeneration used for removing scars

TELL ME MORE!
One type of cell (which create scars) are changed into another type of cell (which does not create scars). This could really help in skin regenerating itself and may have other uses too, including stopping wrinkles from appearing!

Your skin is made from cells, billions of them. These are built up of layers, like an onion. Your skin is thinnest on your eyelids. It's thickest on your feet and the palms of your hands because these places get more wear and tear. The epidermis is your skin's outer layer. There are no blood vessels here and the cells on the very outside are already dead, with about 40,000 falling off you every minute!

DIFFERENT TYPES OF CELLS CAN BE FOUND IN THE EPIDERMIS.

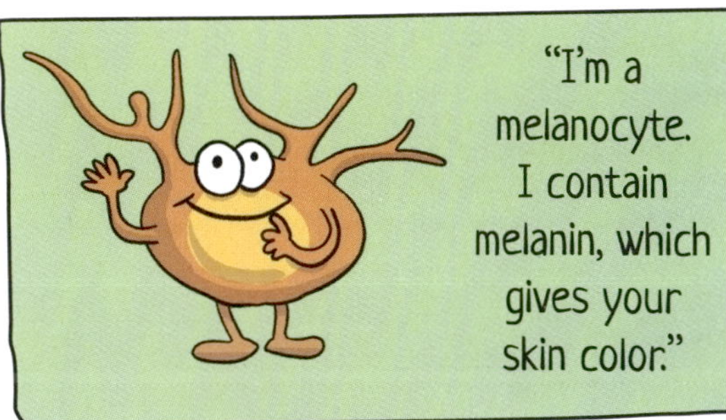

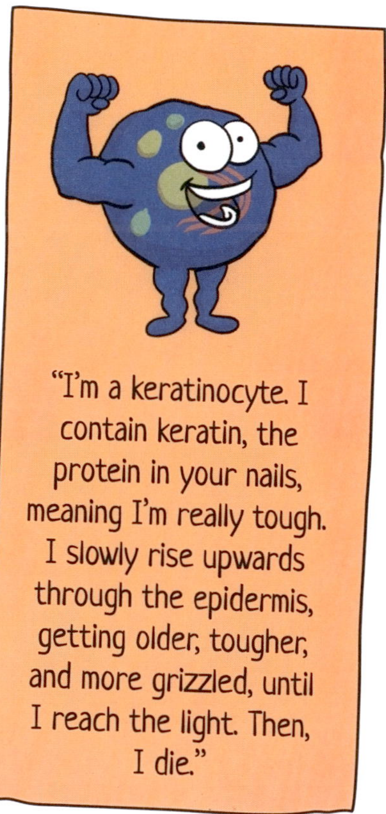

THE DERMIS LIES UNDERNEATH THE EPIDERMIS.

It's a busy place, full of millions of sweat glands and oil glands, hair follicles (where your hairs grow from) and about 17 km (11 miles) of blood vessels. The cells here make proteins that keeps your skin stretchy.

The dermis also gives you fingerprints.

Tiny oil glands attached to hair follicles make an oily product called sebum*. These glands are found everywhere, except the soles of the feet and the palms of the hand, but you have lots on your head.

*Yes, I know, it sounds like see-bum. And yes, that's a little bit funny.

SO, WHAT DOES THE SEBUM DO?

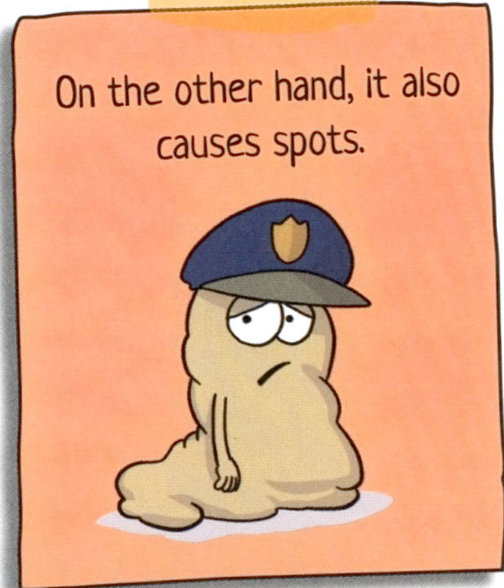

WHAT ABOUT SWEAT?

Three million or so sweat glands help you to stay cool. By releasing sweat, you can keep your body at a healthy temperature and stop it overheating. More sweat is made when you exercise, which is why you need to drink more water when you run around or play sport. Everybody has slightly different sweat from other people. You even make different sweat in different situations.

Your sweat contains more proteins when you are stressed or scared.

Your normal sweat, produced when you run, contains water and salt.

Unless you're running from something scary, then it might be a mixture of both.

The last layer is the hypodermis. About half of this consists of fat tissue, which helps keep you warm, helps cushion your body, and acts as an energy reserve. It also makes a hormone called leptin which controls hunger. A stretchy protein attaches to the muscles underneath the skin.

HOW DOES SKIN HEAL?

Let's explore what might happen if you suffer...

A Painful Paper Cut!

STEP 1:

You're reading your favorite book (... maybe this one?) You run a finger lovingly down the side of a page, considering the wise words and... ouch! The page has cut you! Blood oozes out.

STEP 2:

You wash and dry the wound, then wrap a plaster around it. You narrow your eyes at the book. Why did it do this? Why?

STEP 3:

Meanwhile, beneath the plaster, tiny platelets flood to the wound, changing shape, sticking together to make a clot. This forms a scab. The wound is sealed.

STEP 4:

It's not over. War rages, white blood cells attack and eat invading bacteria. The tissue around the wound reddens and swells. When the battle's done, the victorious cells signal their victory. Keratinocytes (tough skin cells) move in.

STEP 5:

Your cells use stretchy proteins to join your skin together, forming a scab. Eventually, the scab falls off, revealing new skin..

Do not pick the scab. Understand? Do. Not. Pick. The. Scab.

This could slow down healing, make the wound bleed, and will make scarring more likely. And definitely don't **pick** the scab and then **eat** it! Euurrghh! Instead, eat food high in protein (fish, pulses, nuts) and vitamins (fruit and vegetables) to help your body heal.

You skin is constantly being battered. It can normally cope but deeper, more serious cuts may need medical help such as stitches or glue. Sometimes, larger injuries leave scars no matter what you do. They can be caused by too much collagen (stretchy protein) being made or the healing not happening in exactly the right place. Scars usually fade over time.

WHY DO PEOPLE HAVE DIFFERENT SKIN COLOR?

Remember the skin cells called melanocytes? It's these cells that give people their skin color. Everybody has a similar number of these cells in their skin, but in darker-skinned people the cells are larger and contain more melanin. Melanin is the stuff that colors your skin, your hair, and the iris (the colored part) of your eyes. Your helpful melanocytes package up the melanin and give it as gifts to other skin cells.

Like many things, your skin color comes from your parents, but it's the result of thousands of years of adaptation. People whose ancestors come from parts of the world where the sun is less bright usually have lighter skin. That's because it's easier to produce vitamin D from sunlight if your skin is less dark. Vitamin D helps your body absorb calcium, and so is very important for keeping your bones strong and healthy.

In sunnier, warmer places in the world, darker skin protects people from getting burnt by bright sunlight. Some people (and some other animals) are born with a condition called **albinism,** which means their bodies do not make melanin at all, giving them very pale skin.

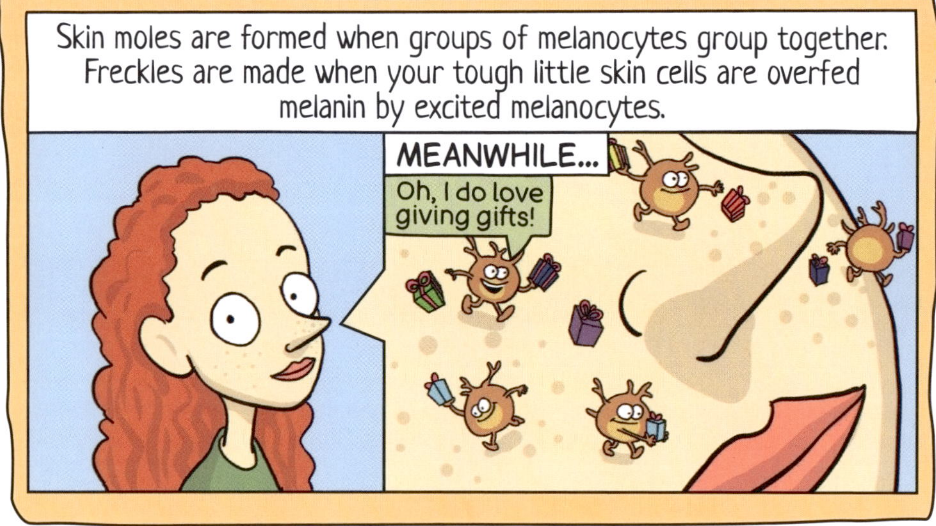

Eating certain fruit or vegetables can also give your skin a healthy golden glow. The yellow, red, and orange pigments in carrots, tomatoes, and oranges are particularly good at doing this. Another reason to eat lots of vegetables!

HAIR IS MADE FROM A PROTEIN CALLED KERATIN.

Hair grows from hair follicles. Your body has about five million of these, and you have about 100,000 follicles on your head. A growing hair looks a bit like a spring onion. In fact, the rounded part under the skin is even called a bulb. Your follicles decide whether your hair will be thick or fine. The shape of a follicle molds each hair, making it straight, wavy, or curly.

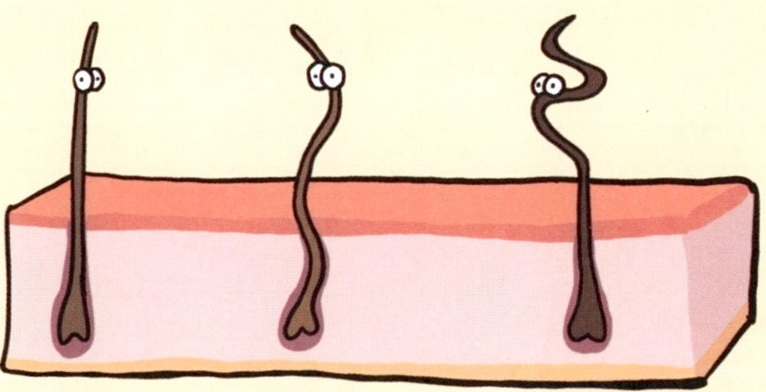

A hair on your head grows for up to six years before it falls out. Every day, you will lose up to 100 head hairs. The good news? Usually, the follicle will soon start growing a new hair.

Only the cells in the root are alive, the hair that you can see is dead. Just as well, otherwise haircuts would be really painful. As cells die, they are pushed out of the follicle and your hair grows. Oily sebum glands keep your hair shiny.

Melanocytes (remember those?) are found in each follicle, giving the growing hair pale or dark melanin or a mixture of both. More dark melanin means darker hair, more pale melanin means lighter colored hair. Your skin gets darker when it's hit by sunlight because your cells make more melanin. Hair, however, gets lighter because there are no living cells to make melanin.

SUNLIGHT + SKIN = DARKER SKIN

SUNLIGHT + HAIR = LIGHTER HAIR

Your hair helps to keep you warm. The hairs in your nose and ears also stop nasty microbes getting inside your body. Hair also stops your skin getting burnt by the sun.

FUN FACT:

Ever had goosebumps? Perhaps when you were cold... or scared? In humans, goosebumps are now pretty useless, However, waaayyy back in the past when our ancestors were hairier and hunted by predators, goosebumps would make the hairs stand on end, helping to trap heat and making the hairy ancestor look bigger and more fearsome.

Unlike other mammals, humans do not have whiskers. Beards are not whiskers, no matter what your beardy uncle might say.

HOWEVER, YOU DO HAVE EXPRESSIVE EYEBROWS WHICH...

- tell other people you are happy, surprised, or sad
- show disbelief at a tall tale
- stop sweat running into your eyes

Humans also have eyelashes. These keep dust and tiny particles out of your eyes. Most people have up to 200 hairs around their upper lid and about 100 around their lower lid. People of Asian heritage usually have thicker eyelashes, while people of European descent usually have more eyelashes. However, this can vary greatly between people within any group.

Your fingernails and toenails are also made from keratin that is really tightly packed in, making it very hard. And just like your hair, the parts that you can see are not alive.

It's in the nail root that all the action is taking place. Here, new cells are constantly being made, shouldering the older ones out of the way and jostling for space. The older cells get harder and harder, until they are thick with keratin, and eventually die. They are pushed out of the root.

FINGERNAILS ARE USEFUL IN SEVERAL WAYS.

- They protect the delicate ends of your soft fingers and toes.
- They help you pick things up.
- They are useful for scratching yourself when you have an itch.

BUT BE AWARE. NAILS ARE TEMPTING THINGS AND CAN LEAD YOU INTO BAD HABITS SUCH AS...

1. Nose picking
2. Nail biting
3. Picking things out from under your nails
4. Eating the things you've picked out from under your nails
5. Making screeching noises down blackboards

Resist temptation. Use your nails only for good.

WHAT ABOUT FINGERPRINTS?

All humans have a huge amount of things in common. Your DNA is mostly the same as everybody else's DNA. Identical twins have exactly the same DNA as each other. That's why they look alike, even though their personalities can be quite different.

But everybody has different fingerprints: *even identical twins.*

There is no one alive who has the same fingerprints as you. No one in the past had the same ones, and — this is the really incredible bit — nobody in the future will have the same ones either.

Your prints are a set of **arches, loops,** and **whorls** that are just yours.

Your fingerprints help you grip onto things (like tree branches or pencils), make your fingertips more sensitive and they are fully formed weeks before you are born. Fingerprinting techniques have been used to catch criminals for over one hundred years.

Apes also have fingerprints. Some chimps and orangutans from zoos in the UK were actually fingerprinted by police in 1975, although they were completely innocent of any crimes.

Koalas and human fingerprints can be very difficult to tell apart. In fact, their prints are so similar that you can only tell them apart if you have the right...

...koala-fication.

Chapter 8:

READY, SET... GROW!

THAT'S IT! YOU'VE MADE A HUMAN!

And you did it in less time than it takes to read a whole book! The good news? You have a new friend! The bad news? There's a few bits and bobs that we haven't mentioned. Don't worry – most of them are parts of other organs (such as the brain) and should already be in place. However, there's a few small-but-very-important parts that you still need to add. Just make sure you pop them in after reading this chapter.

And these busy little parts have a big impact. Even when you're sitting still, your body is full of action. Cells are dying and dividing. Invaders are being fought off and destroyed. Your organs are doing their thing quietly, without making any fuss about it (usually you're not even aware of what they're doing, though you would notice if they stopped doing it). And these busy little parts have a big impact. Even when you're sitting still, your body is full of action. Usually, things are just ticking along nicely.

But sometimes there's a lot more going on, as you'll see later...

HUMANS LIVE A LONG TIME

We may also be the only animals who are aware that we age. Let's take a look at the sort of things scientists have been doing to help us live long and healthy lives.

BREAKTHROUGH:
Destroying zombie cells used for – huh? Zombie cells?

TELL ME MORE!
Cells are usually very well behaved. They do their thing, multiply a number of times, and, when their times comes, they die. However, some cells just don't play by the rules. So-called "zombie cells" stop multiplying (which is just as well), but then refuse to die. Instead, they cause swelling by releasing nasty chemicals. Drugs are being developed that'll take 'em out!

BREAKTHROUGH:
AI used for developing new medicines.

TELL ME MORE!
Yep, it's our trusty friend AI, which is brilliant at spotting patterns. So brilliant that it's being used to look at different drugs, working out which ones would work best, including drugs that kill zombie cells!

BREAKTHROUGH:
Discovering Klotho protein used for staying healthy for longer

TELL ME MORE!
Klotho is a protein named after a god-like being from Greek mythology. She (the god, not the protein) and her sisters controlled the length of people's lives by weaving and cutting threads. Your body makes the protein klotho naturally. Scientists believe it may help you live longer and also protect your organs, such as your kidneys, brain, and lungs, from disease.

BREAKTHROUGH:
Keyhole Surgery used for quick-healing operations.

TELL ME MORE!
A surgeon works through a small cut during an operation whilst another even tinier cut is made so that a really tiny camera* can be inserted. The surgeon gets to see what they're doing (very important) and the wounds heal quickly afterwards. Very useful if there's anything you need to take out... or add in.

*Think needle sized! Scientists are also trying to develop tiny cameras which could be swallowed (by patients, not scientists) and then travel around the body!

SO HOW DOES YOUR BODY KNOW HOW TO GROW?

Well, there's a simple answer and a complicated answer..
simple answer: DNA. **Complicated answer:** Deoxyribonucleic acid.

You may remember meeting DNA briefly back in chapter one. The fact is, DNA is like a very thick recipe book for telling our bodies how to grow and how to function. You get this recipe book from your parents. DNA determines your eye and skin color and has a big impact on other things, such as your height, how sporty you are, and how healthy you will be.

Your genome is the whole recipe book of your DNA, and it is completely unique. Nobody alive has the same genome as you. Nobody in the past had the same genome, and nobody in the future will either. Unless you have an identical twin, of course. Then your DNA will be the same.

FUN FACT:
Svante Pääbo received a Nobel Prize in 2022 for his work on genomes. He looked at our distant relatives, including Neanderthals, an extinct type of human that died out thousands of years ago. He discovered that many modern humans have some Neanderthal DNA!

Your genome is divided into different chromosomes. You have 46 chromosomes altogether, coming in 23 pairs (each pair consists of one chromosome from each parent). Some chromosomes are longer than others and include more information on them. Sections on each chromosome contain instructions for making proteins

THESE SECTIONS OF YOUR CHROMOSOMES ARE CALLED GENES.

Confused? Well, it is quite complicated. Maybe it'll help to think of it like this...

Genome:
the whole recipe book

Chromosome:
one of the 23 chapters in the book (each chapter covers a pair of chromosomes)

Gene:
one of the recipes

YOUR DNA INCLUDES OVER 20,000 GENES.

Each chromosome is made up of tightly wound spools of DNA, which is organized into something called a double helix. Imagine two threads twisting round and round each other. There are 3 billion pairs of genes in these strings (that's 6 billion altogether), with each one given the letter C, G, A, or T. If you read one letter per second, it would take you about 100 years to read out your whole genome!

There are so many letters that if you arranged your DNA into one long thread and held it up, it would be taller than you at 1.8 m (6 ft) long. Not that you could see it, as it is much thinner than a human hair!

WE ARE MADE FROM TRILLIONS OF CELLS.

But cells do not live forever, and we are constantly replacing ones that die. We also need more cells when we are growing. How does this happen?

Well, it's something called cell mitosis. This is when a cell divides. No, it doesn't mean the cell does some math. It means that the cell splits in two. **Cells divide to make more cells:**

"Hi. I'm a stem cell. I can divide myself to make more stem cells or I can turn myself into a few different types of cell."

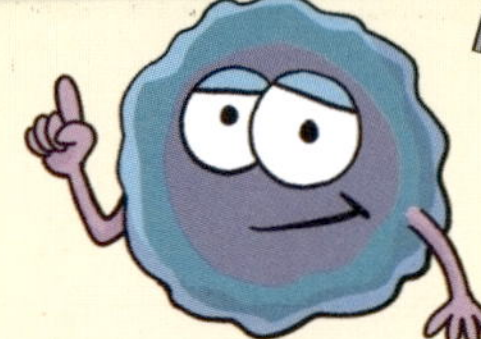

"Hello. I'm not a stem cell, but we do look very similar! I can only make a copy of myself."

Cells spend their time resting, doing the stuff they're supposed to do (like making proteins), or dividing. Cells in your body divide if they receive the right message.

A CELL DIVIDES ITSELF BY:

- copying every chromosome (the sausage-like sections of DNA)
- doubling up its organelles (the bits inside, like the nucleus)
- getting bigger
- splitting in two

Most cells divide about 50 times before they're worn out. Stem cells continue for longer but, eventually, even they get tired. You see, every time a cell copies itself, it loses a tiny bit of DNA from the end of each chromosome. At first, this isn't a problem as chromosomes have some extra end bits, but over time these become too short, and a cell dies.

Some cells, known as gametes or sex cells, only have half the number of chromosomes, 23 instead of the normal 46 that other cells have. That's because there's a possibility they will pair up with another cell (also with 23 chromosomes) and make the 46 that most humans have.

We'll take a look at that later.

HOW DOES YOUR BODY KNOW WHAT IS GOING ON IN OTHER PARTS OF YOUR BODY?

That's where the **endocrine system comes in**. No, the endocrine system is not a collection of planets in a faraway galaxy. But it is a collection of glands and organs that make hormones. Hormones are chemical messages which are sent around the body. When they get to the right type of cell (and only the right type), they deliver the message. This is because they only "attach" to that type of cell and ignore others.

The message might tell cells to:

- make a protein
- keep hold of something
- let something go
- or start making copies of themselves

It works a bit like this... Your hypothalamus (part of your brain) organises your pituitary gland, which releases hormones to tell other parts of your body what to do.

THERE ARE PLENTY MORE GLANDS:

Your thyroid also produces a hormone important in growing. If it makes too much, you'll end up skinny and a bit sweaty, but too little can lead to tiredness and a slow heartbeat, so it's important it gets it right.

Your body is packed full of hormone-making glands and organs.

Your pineal gland makes a hormone that helps you sleep.

Your adrenal glands perch one on each kidney, like little hats. They make several hormones, including adrenaline which helps you respond quickly to danger.

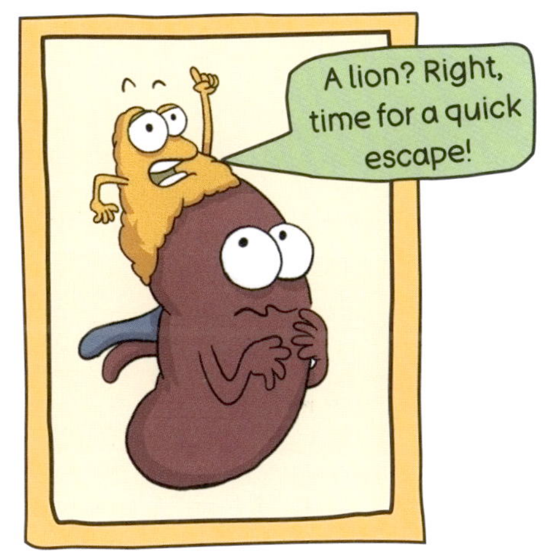

Your pancreas makes one hormone that tells the liver to release sugar and another called insulin which tells the liver to store sugar. A condition called diabetes happens when the pancreas does not make enough insulin (Type I diabetes) or when the body does not respond to the insulin (Type II diabetes).

Your heart releases a hormone to tell the kidneys to take extra water out of your blood. Your kidneys release a hormone to tell your bone marrow to produce more red blood cells. Even the fat cells in your body release a hormone to tell the brain whether you need to eat or not.

MALES AND FEMALES ALSO HAVE DIFFERENT GLANDS THAT PRODUCES HORMONES.

Females have ovaries, which are a type of sex gland. There are two of these inside the body. When the pituitary gland sends a message, the ovaries produce hormones that control what a female's body does during puberty. Ovaries also provide a home for a female human's thousands of egg cells.

Males have two testes which sit outside the body in their own sac (so they don't get too hot!) These sex glands produce a hormone which helps to develop bone and muscle strength. They also produce sperm, a cell produced by males when they reach puberty. Each of these sperm cells has a long tail used for swimming.

THERE ARE OTHER DIFFERENCES TOO:

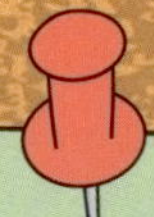

Females have:

- a uterus, where a baby develops
- a vulva, or outside sex parts
- a vagina, which connects the vulva with the uterus
- fallopian tubes, which connect the ovaries to the uterus

Males have:

- a penis, or outside sex parts
- a scrotum, the sac that contains the testes
- a prostate gland, which produces a fluid to help sperm swim*

*kicks into action during puberty!

THE STORY OF THE EGG AND SPERM

An egg cell is much bigger than a sperm cell, but when they meet, they might join together.

Egg cells and sperm cells only have 23 chromosomes each. The sperm cell pushes its way through the outer layer of the egg cell, to create a cell with a full set of chromosomes. This is called a zygote, or a fertilized cell, with the potential to become an entirely new human being. Half of its chromosomes are from one parent, half from the other. The new cell soon splits into two cells, which then divide into four cells, then eight, then sixteen, and so on. This division continues and, after seven days, the zygote is actually visible to the human eye. It's about the size of this full stop.

After about 14 days, some stem cells turn into other cells, like heart or skin cells. The DNA gives a sort of map, or recipe, on how the little life-form should develop. Along the way some odd things happen, including...

- growing a tail (which is later absorbed)
- growing hair (which is usually lost before birth)
- growing a skeleton of cartilage (which is later replaced by bone)

But gradually, over about 280 days or so, one cell becomes a trillion. It also becomes many different types of cell (more than 200, in fact). And during this time, the developing baby is completely dependent on its mom for everything: food, water, oxygen, and getting rid of the waste products. The experiences that the baby gets during this time are really important.

For example, females who eat carrot or kale while pregnant have babies that usually like carrot or kale!

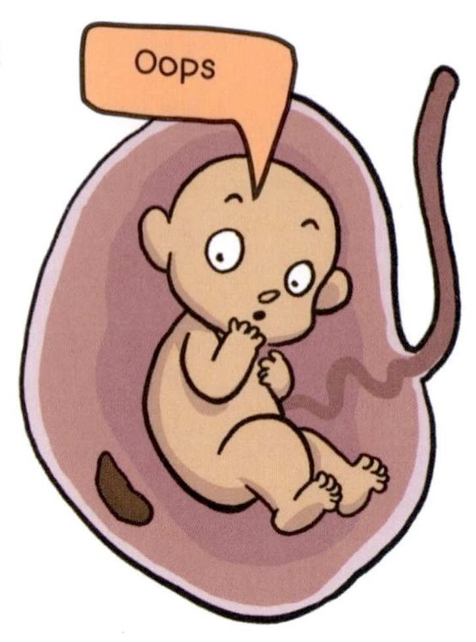

When a baby is born, there are many things it cannot do. A newborn baby can only focus on objects about 10 cm (4 in) away. Any further than that, and things get blurry! They cannot walk, or speak, or ride a bike. It takes them at least 8 weeks to realise their hands belong to them!

Built to survive? Hardly.

So why are baby humans so useless? Many baby animals can walk soon after being born and even those that can't, such as gorillas, can grip onto their parents.

WELL, THERE'S GOOD REASONS FOR ALL OF THIS.

1. Humans walk upright (unlike other apes). This allows us to walk and run longer distances but has meant our bodies changed shape over millions of years. Our hips have grown narrower, making it more difficult for women to give birth to large babies.

2. Babies have large heads because humans have large brains. They might not be ready for the world, but they are ready to learn!

3. Humans are social! Like most other apes, we are meant to live in groups, so there's always somebody to look after the babies!

But, babies are learning from day one, figuring out how humans interact with each other. It takes a baby about six months before it can sit up, nine months before it can crawl, and a year before it can walk. But during all that time, the neurons in a baby's brain are already hard at work. Connections are being made and pathways are being strengthened. Babies might not be able to talk but they understand.

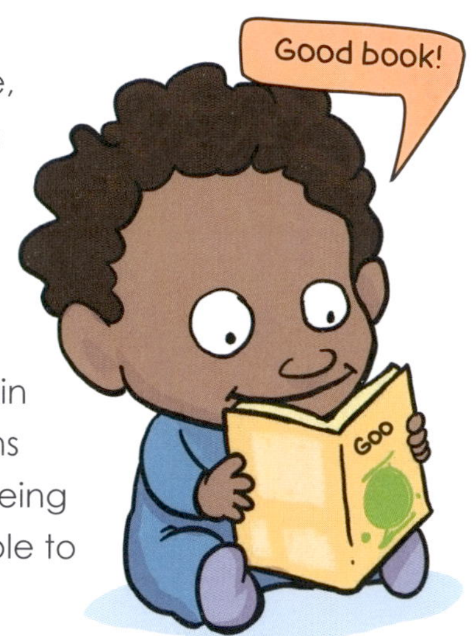

Well, understand more than they can say, which isn't saying a lot.

YOUR BODY IS CONSTANTLY CHANGING.

During childhood, your cells busily multiply, allowing you to grow. New bone cells make your bones longer, new skin cells allow more room for everything to grow, new... you get the idea.

Puberty is the big change on your journey to becoming an adult. It happens at different ages for different people, depending on when your body decides it is ready. It starts with your hypothalamus telling your pituitary gland to send a hormone to your ovaries or testes.

THIS HORMONE KICK-STARTS OTHER THINGS, INCLUDING...

- your liver telling your muscles and the cartilage at the end of your bones to grow
- your body growing more hair, including in your armpits and pubic regions (where your sex organs are)
- spots or acne, caused by these extra hormones

During puberty, females develop breasts, their uterus gets larger, and their hips grow wider. Females normally have their first period (when the body releases an egg) around 12 years of age. These usually become more regular until they're happening every four weeks or so.

Males' testes grow larger, as do their muscles, their ribs, shoulders, and other bones. Their voice box gets bigger and their vocal cords thicker, making their voices deeper.

It doesn't end there! Some scientists believe that your brain won't be fully developed until you are about 25 years old!

As we age, our cells get worse at copying themselves and making proteins. Some cells stop repairing tissues as quickly, whilst other get messier, or lazier. Some die and are not replaced.

For example, humans start with about 15,000 cells in each ear covered in tiny hairs. These hairs vibrate, allowing you to hear. But loud sounds can damage these hairs, making hearing worse.

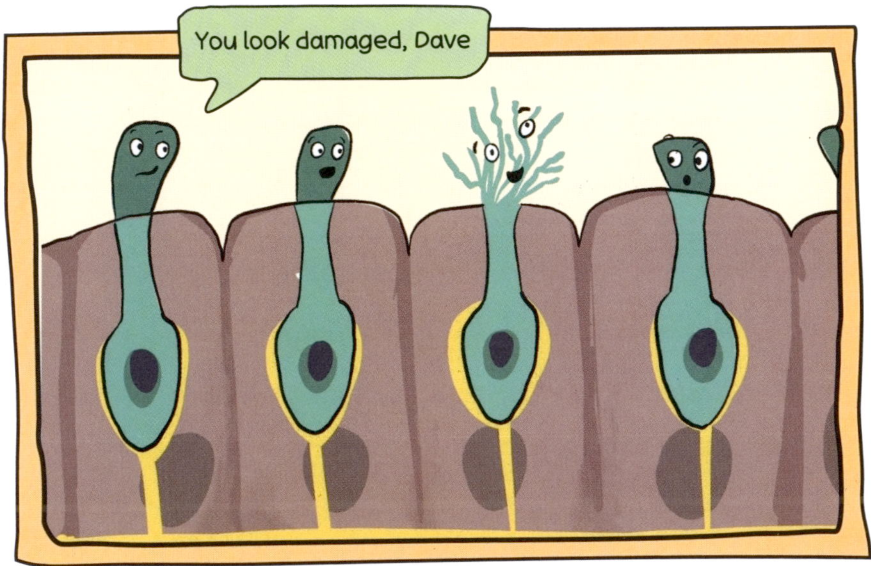

And once they're damaged, they can't be replaced.

Change can be scary, but these changes are natural. Talk to someone you trust if you have any worries about what might happen.

Chapter 9:

STAYING ALIVE!

Your body is truly amazing, but there are still a lot of things that can wrong. Let's take a look at some of the cutting-edge science being developed right now to help our bodies be the best they can be:

BREAKTHROUGH:

CAR T-cells used for giving cells superpowers

TELL ME MORE!

Imagine if you could take cells from a person's body, change them, and then put them into somebody else's body to fight disease. Well, that's exactly what's happened! In London's Great Ormond Street hospital, children with leukaemia (a type of cancer that affects the blood) have been given T-cells that have been "improved" so they are better at destroying cancerous cells.

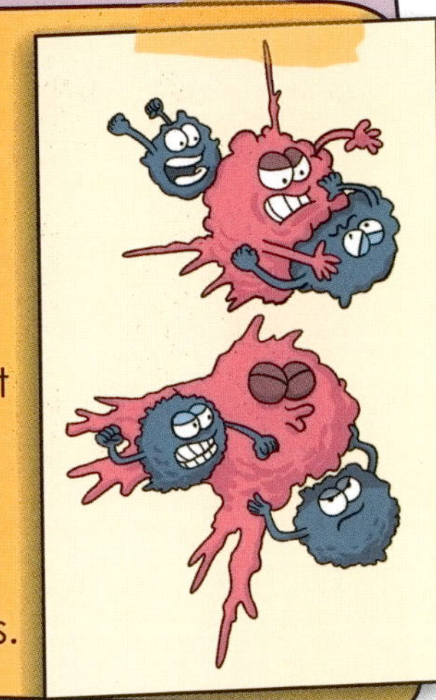

BREAKTHROUGH:

Quantum dots used for finding cancer, delivering medicines, and mapping the brain.

TELL ME MORE!

Wow, quantum dots! Sounds very science-fiction, doesn't it? These mini crystals are a type of nanotechnology with all sorts of possible uses, including taking drugs to the exact place they are needed and showing doctors precisely where cancer might be in a patient's body.

WHAT CAUSES ALLERGIES?

Your white blood cells are constantly hunting for nasties and for cells that aren't doing the right thing.

But sometimes our immune systems get it wrong. Our white blood cells meet something harmless and start a war. It's like you seeing a squirrel in your garden and calling in the army.

Some of these allergens – pollen, pet fur, dust mite poo (yes, really!) – cause our bodies to overreact. There are medicines called antihistamines that calm things down, while nose sprays flush away the problem.

Immunotherapy is where tiny amounts of an allergen are given to a patient so their body gets used to it.

Anaphylaxis is a very serious reaction to a food, medicine, or insect sting. An injection of adrenaline (a hormone that speeds up breathing and heart rate) is often enough to stop the reaction.

HOW DO WE FIGHT DISEASES?

Let's start by looking at vaccination. This is where your body is given a tiny amount of a disease, and your white blood cells meet it and learn how to destroy it. A vaccine can make you a little bit poorly for a day or two, but that's better than getting the full version of the disease!

There are vaccines for all sorts: measles, mumps, tetanus, polio – all of which can be pretty nasty if you get them. The measles vaccine alone is estimated to save nearly one million lives each year!

Hundreds of years ago, smallpox killed lots of people. In 1796, Edward Jenner created the first smallpox vaccine.* In 1980, The World Health Organisation (WHO) said there was no more smallpox – it had been eradicated.

*He did it in an icky way: injecting pus from a milkmaid's sore (she had cow pox, which is similar to smallpox) into an eight-year-old boy. Yeuch!

Antibiotics kill bacteria. The first antibiotic was discovered by Alexander Fleming in 1928. He called it penicillin. There are now over one hundred different types, and they have saved millions of lives.

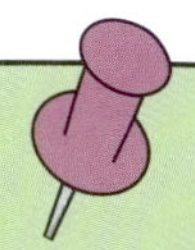

Let's take a look at antibiotics, using...

FOUR FACTS AND A FIB!

Can you spot the made-up fib lurking among the true facts?

1) Antibiotics only kill harmful bacteria and leave your helpful gut bacteria unharmed.

2) Some bacteria are becoming resistant to antibiotics...

3) ... and it's getting harder to find new antibiotics!

4) Some antibiotics can have side effects, including rashes and mood swings.

5) Some people are allergic to penicillin.

Answer: Number 1 is false. Unfortunately, they kill all bacteria, good and bad alike. This means your gut bacteria need replacing after taking antibiotics.

You can help out by only taking antibiotics when you need them and making sure you finish any medicines you are given. Antibiotics do not work on viruses, such as a cold or the flu. Instead, there are antivirals which kill viruses.

Ever had a fever when you're ill? This is when your body gets hot and sweaty. Your body might deliberately do this to kill nasties inside it!

Being ill is part of being alive. Sometimes you really do need medicine, but illnesses are actually good for your immune system. As the philosopher Friedrich Nietzsche said...

What doesn't kill me makes me stronger.

Although he said it in German, so it didn't sound quite the same.

The placebo effect is a bit weird. In most medical trials where new drugs are tested, half the people taking part are given the real drug (often a tablet), while the other half taking part are given a placebo (a tablet which looks the same, but does absolutely nothing).

This is where it gets strange. People taking the placebo often say that they feel better, even though the tablet shouldn't have any effect! Many feel better even when they know they're taking a placebo.

And why does it work? No one's entirely sure, but it might be due to meeting other people during a trial. The placebo effect does not cure diseases, but it can be used to help control pain.

OUT OF CONTROL CELLS

Most cells multiply. It's part of being a cell. But sometimes cells keep making copies of themselves without stopping, ignoring messages from the body telling them to quit. They multiply out of control and steal oxygen from healthy cells, causing damage to body organs. This is known as cancer.

Cancers can be caused by eating a poor diet, or smoking, or being exposed to too much radiation or sunlight, but some people do all of the right things and still get cancer. Scientists and doctors use different methods to kill cancerous cells.

1) X-ray beams, which are aimed at the cancer

2) A small piece of radioactive metal, which is implanted near the cancer

3) Radioactive liquids, which are put into the body to target the cancer

Chemotherapy uses drugs to kill cancerous cells. Other body parts are also affected, but these usually recover when treatment is stopped.

PLANTS MAKE THEIR OWN FOOD. ANIMALS DO NOT.

You're making a cheese and tomato sandwich. The bread comes from wheat (grown by a plant), the butter and the cheese from a cow (which gets its energy from plants), and the tomato comes from a plant. We may not be able to make food (growing it really isn't the same thing) but we need it to survive. Food gives us essential nutrients that we cannot do without.

"Hi there, I'm a carbohydrate. I'm found in things like bread, potatoes, rice, and pasta, and I give you the energy to move and ponder important questions, like 'what should I have in this delicious sandwich?'"

"Protein here. I'm vital for building strong muscles, keeping healthy tissues, and making hormones in your body. I'm found in meat, eggs, beans, tofu, and more."

"Oh, hi buddy! Nice to meet you! I'm fat and you need me as an important back-up energy source. I also do other things too, like keeping your cells and your brain healthy. I turn up in all sorts of foods: nuts, seeds, olives, oily fish. Be careful though: some unsaturated* fats are good for you, while some aren't quite as healthy."

*Unsaturated fats are an important part of a healthy diet. Saturated fats (found in meat, dairy products, and palm oil) are okay if you don't eat too much, but trans fats (found in cakes, biscuits, pies, fried foods, and in some meat and dairy products) should only be eaten in very small amounts.

That's not all! Your body also needs...

VITAMINS AND MINERALS.

Small amounts keep your body in good working order:

- vitamin A helps you fight infection
- vitamin D helps your body absorb calcium
- vitamin K helps with healing (yep, there's a vitamin K, but no F, G, H, I, or J)
- calcium keeps bones and teeth healthy
- iron allows red blood cells to carry oxygen around your body

WATER:

You need water to keep your blood flowing, help to flush out waste, and stay cool. Your body loses water when you breathe out, when you sweat, and when you go to the toilet, and you should drink about six to eight glasses of water a day to replace this. A lot of water comes in food, especially fruit and vegetables.

Oh, don't mind me...

FIBER:

Fiber helps to help keep your digestive system working properly! A lack of fiber can cause constipation (where it's difficult to do a poo). Eat plenty of whole grains like brown rice, as well as beans, and fruit and vegetables to avoid this!

It's important to keep a balanced diet, full of lots of different foods which give your body everything it needs. Many countries recommend eating five portions of different fruits and vegetables a day (you can't just eat five apples). That's about 400 g (0.9 lbs) a day for an adult, or a cat-sized amount of fruit and vegetables every 10 days!

WHAT IS METABOLISM?

Good question, and I thought you'd never ask! Your metabolism is the chemical reactions happening inside your body as it makes use of all the food you've eaten.

LET'S MEET THE TWO PROCESSES INVOLVED:

CATABOLISM

Tell us more:

"I am the great destroyer! Strong. Invincible! My valiant warriors - the enzymes - break food down into sugars, proteins, fats, and other stuff. Enzymes are a type of protein that speed up stuff happening."

If we were talking about cats, we'd be discussing cat catabolism! Hah!

ANABOLISM

Tell us more:

"Well, you see, catabolism is about destroying stuff. What I do is much harder. I take those little bits and bobs and put them together to make new things. I also use enzymes, but different ones than catabolism."

I have this friend Anna. Well, if we were talking about me getting on with stuff inside her body, we'd be discussing Anna's anabolism. He he he!

WHY DO WE SLEEP?

You'll probably spend about eight hours a day, or a third of your life, asleep. Babies and children need even more sleep, and teenagers can spend up to half the day in bed. People *can* survive without sleep for longer (the world record is over 11 days without nodding off) but not getting enough sleep can lead to problems such as depression, high blood pressure, moodiness, and poor decision making.

So, sleep is good for you, though scientists are puzzled about why exactly. But, like always, those clever scientists have some clever ideas:

1. Sleep helps you remember things (dreaming may also help)
2. Sleep gives your body a chance to wash your brain. The cells in your brain contract slightly and liquid washes away waste, as well as any lurking nasties
3. Sleep gives your body a chance to grow (your pituitary gland releases more growth hormone during sleep)
4. It stops you using energy
5. It resets your mood

Sleep is controlled by your hypothalamus. As the sun goes down, your eyes tell your brain the light is changing, and your hypothalamus tells your pineal gland to make more melatonin. Your body gets you ready to sleep by lowering your temperature and making you drowsy.

WHY DO WE DREAM?

There are five different stages of sleep and your body repeats those stages several times during a long sleep. One of the stages is called REM (Rapid Eye Movement) and this is when you dream. Your brain is very active during REM sleep, but your muscles are relaxed, which stops you acting out your dreams.

DREAMING MAY HELP YOU:

1. process emotions and experiences (e.g. meeting a lion)
2. solve problems (e.g. run away from the lion)
3. become more creative (e.g. thinking about how else the lion could have been avoided)

Dreaming can be incredibly helpful. In fact, many great thinkers claim to have had great thoughts during dreams

The writer of this book dreamt about elephants attaching springs to their feet so they could bounce around like kangaroos. Best idea in a dream ever or what? (Elephants can't actually jump, so maybe not such a good idea?)

WHY DO WE SNORE?

Snoring is a habit that some people have when they are asleep. It happens when the tongue falls backward, and the throat muscles relax. This means there is less space for air to enter the lungs. When the sleeper breathes in, parts of the throat vibrate causing the snoring sounds.

Snoring is very, very annoying.

And that's it! You've reached the end of the book. Now you know everything that goes into building a human and keeping it alive!

Doesn't your brain feel MASSIVE now? Well, I don't know about you, but after all that learning, I think it's time to take a snooze...

TOMORROW'S WORLD

Tomorrow's World is an exciting series that takes readers on an unforgettable journey into the core of the coolest sciences our world has **EVER** seen.

From the wonders of space and the depths of the oceans to the exciting possibilities of AI and the risks of an asteroid hitting Earth (gulp), this series is overflowing with fascinating facts and comic-style illustrations, showing how scientists around the world are constantly shaping (and saving) our future.

Written by renowned authors and reviewed by specialists in the field, each book is a perfect blend of fun, adventure, and of course, a fart joke or two.

This series inspires young readers to not just dream big, but to dream of tomorrow. **The future of science begins here!**